Willie's Chocolate Factory

COOKBOOK

WILLIE HARCOURT-COOZE

HODDER &
STOUGHTON

First published in Great Britain in 2009 by Hodder & Stoughton
An Hachette UK company
First published in paperback in 2010

1

A CIP catalogue record for this title is available from the British Library

ISBN 978 0 340 98040 8

Photography © Cristian Barnett

Design by willwebb.co.uk

Typeset in Rockwell and Grocer's Script
Printed and bound in Italy by L.E.G.O. Spa

Hodder & Stoughton policy is to use papers that are natural, renewable
and recyclable products and made from wood grown in sustainable forests.
The logging and manufacturing processes are expected to conform to the
environmental regulations of the country of origin.

Hodder & Stoughton Ltd
338 Euston Road
London NW1 3BH

www.hodder.co.uk

For my father

Contents

The Story

The Recipes

Introduction

Cacao has taken centre stage during the last fifteen years of my life. My adventures, in Venezuela and Devon, in the pursuit of the finest beans in the world have been incredible. When I left London in the early 1990s to follow my dreams on the other side of the world, I never imagined that I'd be able to share them with so many people.

This collection of recipes, stories and memories reflect those often difficult years of travel, farming and production. Languid tropical evenings inspired Tania's and my early experimentation combining cacao with the rich harvests of fruit and vegetables that grew at our hacienda. Cloud Forest Cake is so named because of the cloud forest sugar that we baked with; cooking with the ingredients that surrounded us first revealed the amazing range of flavours, sweet and savoury, that cacao creates when used as a condiment.

I want this book to act as an enduring point of reference for all culinary adventurers who are open to this possibility of placing a bar of top quality cacao alongside the salt, pepper, chillies and garlic that sit by the side of the oven. The recipes included here may surprise some readers – but yes you can enhance a Pumpkin and Red Pepper Soup with cacao, and infusing vodka with roasted cacao nibs will give a Bloody Mary a brilliant kick!

One day I hope that people will become connoisseurs who treat chocolate like wine – that they will educate their palettes to recognise that there are differences in the quality of chocolate as extreme as the differences between sparkling wine and champagne! The chocolate bar you pick up at the newsagent is unlikely to even hint at the wonderful possibilities of flavour, but have a go at creating some of these dishes and hopefully you might begin to understand what a remarkable and transformative ingredient cacao can be.

I would like you to come on a journey with me as I seek out the haciendas of South America that are producing some of the most phenomenal beans in the world – stopping at nothing to spread the word about the highest quality cacao that can be tasted. Neither the recipes nor stories can stand alone: cooking, living in Venezuela and setting up the factory in Devon are all inseparable elements of our life with cacao. It's the icing on my cloud forest cake that by reading this book you can experience some of these moments with me…

Saludos, Willie

Chapter 1

El Tesoro: Coming Home

I discovered the Hacienda El Tesoro by obeying the first rule of adventure, which is to follow all tangents, paths and possibilities.

It was February 1994; Tania and I were exploring the Venezuelan Andes with her sister Sophie, travelling mainly on horseback and living on the tasty fat trout that I caught in mountain lakes along the way. After a few weeks, we came to Laguna Negra, a lake on the edge of a little town called Santo Domingo. There, we ran into Carlos, a Colombian artist who painted pictures for an Andean timeshare hotel.

One night, as we were sitting by our campfire under the stars, sharing bottles of rum and enjoying the beautiful surroundings, Carlos suddenly leapt to his feet. 'You love the mountains?' he said excitedly. 'Then you have to go to where the mountains meet the sea!'

'Where's that?' I asked.

'Choroni!' he replied. '*Hombre*, you must see that place!'

A few days later, we moved on from Santo Domingo. Where to next? we wondered. In an instant, Carlos's words came back to me.

'Choroni!' I said. 'Where the mountains meet the sea.'

We followed the tangent. Arriving in the remote coastal town of Choroni one hot steamy tropical morning in February, we headed straight for the beach, a wide crescent of golden sand backed by swaying coconut palms. Enclosed by a steep range of forested mountains, the landscape was just as Carlos had described it. Miraculous.

It wasn't long before we got chatting to Mervyn, who rents umbrellas on the beach in Choroni. He seemed like a nice guy; he fancied Tania's sister and invited us for supper. We followed the tangent.

Over black beans and fish, Mervyn told us about Fernando, his close friend and neighbour, who owned a cocoa farm in the lush national park that rose steeply up the mountain behind the town. Fernando was getting older, Mervyn said, and his children weren't really interested in the farm, so he was selling up. Would we like to go and see it?

We thought, how exciting! This will take us up to the cloud forest and the jungle. It was the perfect opportunity to explore the area. Once again, we followed the tangent.

Tania and I never intended to buy a cacao farm in Venezuela, but the

moment we saw the Hacienda El Tesoro we knew we wanted to live there. I remember walking down the rough track to the river and crossing the little footbridge that leads to the main house. It felt like we were passing into another world: a magical place, untouched by the modern age and teeming with life and natural beauty.

My senses came alive as I drank in the sights, sounds and smells of the forest. I had the strangest feeling that somehow I belonged here, that in some way I was coming home. I glanced over at Tania. Her face was glowing with curiosity and delight, her eyes bright with wonder. I reached for her hand and squeezed it. What a brilliant adventure.

Looking up at the pods on the cacao trees, and above them into the multi-coloured canopy of the shade trees, I thought, WOW! My imagination had already been captured by a passage in our guidebook saying that the best cacao in the world grew in this region, but now I could see that there was a whole eco-system up there above the cacao, let alone the cacao itself! Just the colours fascinated me.

There was a moist coolness in the air as we walked through the trees towards the rambling hacienda and patio. Then, suddenly, we broke out of the forest into the sunlight. Everything seemed to blaze with colour, from the emerald green lawn in front of the house to the tall fruit tree to my right, which was heavy with big ripe oranges hanging from every branch. As I took in our wider surroundings and the view of the lush forested valley beneath us, I felt almost dizzy. It was breathtaking.

El Tesoro's owner, Fernando Perreira, emerged from the main house to greet us; he turned out to be a lovely white-haired man of mixed African-Spanish descent. We shook hands and I thanked him for allowing us to come to see the hacienda. 'It's unbelievably beautiful!' I said.

Fernando was passionate about the farm; he had fallen in love with it as a boy and vowed to buy it when he grew up. His eyes lit up as he recounted its history, which dates back to 1640.

As well as the hacienda and patio, there was a large workshop containing a 600-kilo copper still, which had once been used to distil *aguardiente*, the first stage of rum. Below the workshop was the oldest building, a seventeenth-century structure that had a cacao-drying patio backing on to the river and a tunnel for storing cacao away from the heat and sun.

Fernando went on to say that his family had initially lived there, but it had

become their holiday house when his children went away to school. Now he was getting too old to keep it on. It was time to sell.

We arranged to come back a couple of days later. That's when Bertillio Araujo, the head worker, walked us all over the farm, which covers a thousand acres and rises into stunningly beautiful cloud forest. We were blown away by the diversity of the plants and animals around us.

We were gone for hours; along the way I asked Bertillio a million questions. What is this tree? Why is sap running down its bark? How long does the fruit take to ripen? Can you eat it? When does this plant flower? What's the name of this bird, that spider, this snake, that forest rat? We spent a long while inspecting the cacao plantation, which was obviously in need of care and attention. One day, I thought, I'll make chocolate using the beans from these pods. I couldn't wait to start experimenting.

It meant a lot to Fernando that I took so much interest in the farm. Years later Bertillio said to me, 'You know, even Fernando never walked the whole farm, in all the years he owned it.' We hacked through paths that no one had gone down for years; by the time we got back to the farmhouse, our machetes were blunt.

Tania and I fell in love with El Tesoro, with its natural beauty, peace and tranquillity. We could also see its commercial potential, as an eco-tourism project as well as a farm. It seemed like the perfect location for an eco-project: just ten degrees north of the equator, the farm sits below the cloud forest in the breathtaking heights of the Henri Pittier National Park, surrounded by bio-diversity so varied that it lays claims to 3 per cent of world's flora and 7 per cent of the world's bird species, as well as the legendary Chuao cacao, the basis of the world's richest chocolate. It seemed like a great time to be moving into eco-tourism, which was still an emerging branch of the travel industry.

The possibility of living in such a beautiful place and at the same time making money from showing it to other people seemed entirely feasible. Back then we didn't realise how much work would be involved in getting around Venezuelan planning permission.

It was already a working farm and I could see lots of room for expansion and development. Since I was brought up to farm, to be in nature, the idea of owning this amazing tract of land sent thrills down my spine. My passion for working the land went back a long way: I'd spent my childhood on a farm in Southern Ireland.

I was brought up by the kind of brown-rice-brown-bread parents that other

people considered nutty in the 1960s. My earliest memory is of when I was two and my mother took me to the only health food shop within miles, which was located within a signal box in Streatham, above the railway station. When the trains went by underneath, the whole shop shook, which was terrifying!

I was three when my father bought Horse Island in Roaring Water Bay off the south-west coast of Ireland. The following year we moved to an old farmhouse on the mainland, opposite the island. Dad's dream was to create a self-sufficient idyll for my mother, my four sisters and me. For years, we grappled with the coastal climate to produce our own eggs, milk, yogurt, cheese, meat, fish, fruit and vegetables. We kept bees for honey and goats for milk and cheese, and raised cattle and sheep to sell.

I spent much of my childhood in Ireland smoking fish, milling flour, making cheese and pickling fruit. I was reeling-in sea trout even before I had learned to ride my first bicycle.

It's amazing to think that Horse Island now has a helicopter pad. Back then it was deserted, apart from our farm and a couple of abandoned villages from the famine days. We had an old house on the island where we occasionally stayed, but usually we went across from the mainland every morning. It took half an hour to get over to the farm by boat, in our small 18-foot punt. When it was time to take the cows to market, we'd strap one on each side of the boat and swim them across to the mainland.

The island spanned around 160 acres and was long and thin in shape, with two large mounds at either end and a dip in the middle. Realising that we needed water in order to farm, my father got out his divining rod, a willow stick, and walked around until it started to twitch. Ping! He found fresh water right in the dip between the two mounds, fifty metres away from the sea. So that's where we dug our well, deep below sea level, and pumped out water for the animals to drink.

The island was riven with copper mines dating back to the Vikings a thousand years ago. Families of otters lived in the ancient shafts that ran in off the beach and led into the heart of the island through rounded doorways. I used to spend hours on a slope above the shore staring down at the otters as they played with their babies on the shingle. We put nets out at night, drifting with them to catch fish, and sometimes we'd hear a loud swirling splash. Later in the evening we'd find a fish head stuck in the net, because an otter had swiped the body. We never minded, though. Fair's fair: we were co-habiting.

I learned to forage at an early age. I often collected shellfish – closheens and mussels – but only in small quantities, just enough for the family to eat. Closheens could only be collected at the lowest of tides, just a couple of moons in the year, so you couldn't gather more than a few. Oysters were introduced; my father bought a thousand and I bought a thousand with my saved-up pocket money. We had an oyster lantern that cost more than the oysters themselves, and after they'd grown, we used to sit in the boat and open and eat oyster after oyster. I don't remember ever selling them.

When mackerel were running, we had a freezer full of fish and we'd each eat a mackerel every night. Even the sheep dogs and Jack Russells had mackerel for supper, mashed up with parata (flaked corn). Our dogs were always incredibly healthy!

I used to strap my fishing rods to my rickety old bicycle and pedal twelve miles over the hills to a reservoir up a mountain called Mount Gabriel, where I fished for trout. In those days, you could fish with worms, bread, whatever you liked; obviously things have changed now.

One afternoon, soon after I arrived there, I found that I'd run out of worms. Since I wasn't going to cycle the twelve miles home for some more, I started looking around for an alternative. Soon I spotted some fat juicy grasshoppers; I stuck a live grasshopper on the line and threw it out. The grasshopper kicked its legs, which made waves under the water and sent out the message, 'Come and eat me!' Within moments I reeled in the biggest trout I'd ever seen.

Meanwhile, on the other side of the reservoir, people could see I was catching all the fish while they were getting nothing. It was all a bit embarrassing. Soon they were strolling over to see what I was up to, but I wasn't about to reveal my secret weapon. That night I went home with six beautiful trout – I baked them simply in foil with lemon and butter, because simple is best when you've got great ingredients.

I learned early on about the value of good quality ingredients. Food is obviously going to be better if you grow your own, make it and cook it yourself. In Ireland we grew everything, including

wheat and barley and oats, which we milled on the back of the tractor; and my mother planted a kitchen garden that overflowed with fruit and vegetables. I was always aware of the chain between growing, making, cooking and eating, especially when it came to Mum's delicious homemade bread, not to mention her amazing bread pudding.

Years later I applied the same principles when it came to making cacao and chocolate: by doing everything myself – by controlling the entire process – I could be sure of producing the best quality cacao. It was then that I fully appreciated everything my parents had taught me when I was young. They were both very inventive, full of energy and ideas. They laid the foundations for where I am today and I'm incredibly grateful to them.

I was always interested in food production. From the age of twelve I was busy making beer, elderflower champagne and elderberry wine, which turned into port. My parents were amazed. All they had done was give me a little winemaking book, and here were the results!

That was the way things were in my family. No one had time to show you how to do things, or do them for you, because they were off doing their own things. Everyone was busy. One of my sisters had an egg incubator and spent her time hatching chicks. There were vegetables to dig up and animals to milk and feed. When I wasn't helping Dad on the farm, I made dandelion root coffee and jams, or harvested field mushrooms or painted the outside of the house. I never stopped; none of us did.

It wasn't just us. We were surrounded by people who were just as passionate as we were about living off the land. Our neighbours, Tom and Giana Ferguson went on to produce fantastic Gubbeen cheese, which is sold everywhere now. Tom gave me my first air rifle and I used to shoot the odd pheasant on the island, just one or two for supper.

Sadly, my father sold the island in the late 1970s. Farming in that climate had proved to be a lot of hard work and the farm was very isolated. As much as things were in abundance in the summer, winters could be a bit bleak. All the same, it was very hard for him to leave.

As for me, I was devastated. Living outdoors and being a part of nature was ingrained in me. I stayed on in Ireland with Dad for a couple of years, and then moved to London on his insistence. He was always stressing the importance of studying and education, but how was I going to adapt to life in England, where supper came from the supermarket?

Reservoir fishing was just one of the disappointments that awaited me in London. It was too much of a concrete experience. For me, it wasn't just a case of catching fish; the ambience had to be right as well. So I didn't bother.

I worked for my exams, but began to dream about travelling the world. In the back of my mind there was the barely formed idea of finding another Horse Island out there, preferably somewhere hot. I had climbed over the side of our boat in the freezing mid-winter to cut tangled rope off the propeller enough times in my life! (You had to do it really quickly or you'd freeze to death in that water.) Tropical was the way forward. The idea of homegrown mangoes and avocados had a romantic pull for me too.

After doing 'O' levels at a crammer, I moved on to sixth form college in West London. Meanwhile, my social life was on the up and I became known for having people round and cooking for them. We had a lot of parties and ate like kings, because I realised early on that the key to being able to keep my energy levels up was to eat well: good wholesome food.

Then something terrible happened when I was halfway through my 'A' levels. I was walking down the Portobello Road on my way home from a club in Westbourne Grove, with a friend, when a group of guys loomed up ahead of us. Before we knew it, we were surrounded and they were demanding money. I refused to give them any; there was a scuffle and they ran off.

Winded, I fought to catch my breath. It felt as if I'd been kicked in the kidneys. But just as I was beginning to feel okay again, my mate noticed that there was blood all down my side. 'Willie, you've been stabbed!' he cried.

I looked down. Red blood was seeping through my T-shirt, all the way down to my belt. I didn't know it then, but a thin stiletto blade had been thrust five or six inches into my back at a downwards angle, barely missing my lung and spleen.

Panicking in case the guys came back, we moved away fast, heading towards my friend's house, which was about half a mile away. I'd lost loads of blood by the time we got there – it was all down my jeans, everywhere. I didn't make it inside the house, just collapsed on the ground outside. I remember hearing sirens blaring and then I lost consciousness.

I woke up in hospital, gasping for breath. The blade had missed my lung, but only just, so there was quite a lot of bruising in the pulmonary area and it was really hard to breathe. I was in hospital for ten days, three of which were spent in intensive care.

Suddenly I felt quite different about life. I'd only done a year of my maths, physics and chemistry 'A' levels, but school seemed futile now and I was finding it really hard to concentrate. I told my college tutor that I was leaving and he tried to dissuade me, but I felt alienated and everything seemed senseless. It was like a coin had been flipped and I couldn't flip it back again. So I dropped out and went travelling. That was the beginning of all my great adventures.

My stepfather Henry had some friends in Australia and he arranged for me to go and work on a sheep station, as a roustabout. I worked bloody hard, but between times I carried out my passion for hunting, gathering and cooking. I'd go trout-fishing in the creeks and catch four or five-pound rainbow trout in tiny little creeks. We'd drop lantern nets with fat tied on into the murky backwaters of the farm and pull up amazing freshwater crayfish – two-kilo monsters – that we'd take home and cook. We used ancient Lee Enfield 303s and Winchester 20-25s to shoot kangaroos, emus and rabbits: it was a paradise for that sort of thing. The hard work was always intermingled with excitement.

But then came another blow: tragically, eight months into my trip I learned that my father was dying. I flew straight home but, much to my sadness and regret, I didn't make it in time to see him before he died.

The events that had gone before – being knifed, wondering what life was all about and going to Australia – had been extremely unsettling, but Dad dying compounded everything and set me on an emotional rollercoaster. I found it devastating and it left me lost. It was a very bad time for all the family.

I was constantly restless and just didn't know what to do next. Our society ill prepares us for death, especially the death of people close to us, and eighteen is a pivotal age to lose a parent. I was fortunate in that I had a great family. They rallied round and somehow we got through it.

After a year or so, I headed off to South America. In those days, there was hardly any organised tourism over there, so you'd find yourself following mad tangents that led to all kinds of unexpected adventures.

This was back in the era of the *Sendero Luminoso* in Peru, when there were frequent kidnappings and nightly curfews at 1am, and they'd bolt you in the bars and nightclubs until 5am if you stayed out too late. The next day you'd come out of a side street and suddenly be faced with troops on one side of the road, opposite anti-government demonstrators on the other. It was a hotspot time.

Inflation was crazy. You'd go to the bank to change a hundred dollar bill and come out with a carrier bag of cash. Later in the day you'd find yourself paying for a meal with a six-inch wad of notes. The local food in Peru was amazing, though. The local taverns held great big Saturday-night parties and I used to go to these huge tents lined with tables and full of people. The beer would be flowing and the food would be brought in and it would be fantastic, fresh ceviche.

In Lima I heard about these French Guyanese nuns who had a convent in Jiron Ica, an old part of the city. They cooked a great dinner for ten dollars and afterwards they came out and sang. That's why you went, because they sang like French angels.

I did a lot of mountain walking with a Swedish character called Tor; we'd go off for days and days, foraging off the land, picking up the odd straggler on the way. One afternoon, halfway up a mountain, Tor turned to me and said, 'Willie, you're crazy like a fox and you fly like an eagle! Yee ha!!!' The air was thin up there. Neither of us were thinking straight.

Looking back, I can see that I was always half searching for somewhere to settle – a place where I'd be happy away from London. But I didn't find it until I went to Venezuela.

Back in London, I became a partner in a project that ended disastrously, with all the partners falling out. My friend Dean Freeman rang me up and said, 'Willie, you need a break!' Dean is a photographer; he was shooting the stills for a Levi's commercial in America and took me along as his assistant.

One of the jobs was in Monument Valley, the other was in San Francisco, and there was a week's gap in between. I immediately rang my friend Tania Coleridge in Los Angeles. 'I need somewhere to crash for a week,' I said. 'Can I stay with you?'

'Of course!' she said.

I had known Tania since we were in our early twenties. We had fancied each other from the moment we met, but nothing had ever developed because we were always with other people. She had been living in Los Angeles for several years, working first as an actress, then designing clubs and restaurants. Now she co-owned a very successful Hollywood restaurant called the T Rooms.

Naturally I asked if she had a boyfriend, to which she replied she did not. She's single! I thought. I leapt on a plane.

I arrived in LA and it was instant love. The job was cancelled, so I was free to stay on for a blissful three weeks. One day I said, 'Look, I can't stay here forever...' There was a long pause. 'What are you thinking?' I asked her.

'Well, maybe, that we should get married,' Tania said. Of course, she doesn't remember now that it was her who asked me!

'I don't really want to go back to England,' I told her.

Fortunately, neither did she. As it happened, she'd had enough of Hollywood: she was in the process of selling her shares in the T Rooms, the lease on her flat had come up, she'd left her boyfriend and her car had been stolen. So we'd both come to the end of a phase in our respective lives and careers. It was perfect timing.

'Why don't we go to South America, to Venezuela?' I suggested. 'I've got a great friend there. Let's go and visit him.'

'Let's go,' she said, without hesitating.

We had a fantastic time. I didn't know Venezuela very well and it was great to explore it with someone, especially when we travelled through the Andes. After nine months, we returned to England to get married. Our wedding was fantastic, but when it was over we couldn't wait to get back to the mountains.

On our second trip to Venezuela, we discovered the Hacienda El Tesoro. Suddenly everything fell into place. There's a long history of settlers from Europe in that area of the country, and we instantly felt at home on the coast and among the Choroni people.

However, we had only a few places to compare it with. We'd spent time in Caracas and travelling through the Andes, but Venezuela is a vast country and there was so much of it we hadn't explored. This was a huge life change we were planning, and we were about to make a major investment. Was Choroni really the best place for us to settle? We needed to know for sure. Figuring that the only way to find out was to check out the rest of the country before we committed ourselves, we headed to Caracas and rented a car.

Over the next few weeks, we drove the length and breadth of Venezuela. Some of the roads were awful back then, especially along the coast. They're better now, because there's been a lot of oil money invested in transport and infrastructure, but in the mid-1990s they weren't so good. Many of the towns we came to had never seen tourists before, because they were virtually inaccessible. The upside of this was that we came across some really beautiful, secluded beaches and had them all to ourselves. Paradise!

But we didn't really want peace and seclusion all the time, did we? The great thing about Choroni was that you had the best of both worlds – it was beautifully quiet and sleepy during the week and then it livened up at the weekends, when all the bars and restaurants opened their doors and filled up with weekend visitors from Caracas. It was a far cry from the little towns along the coast, where sometimes you felt a bit like a character in a Sergio Leone film

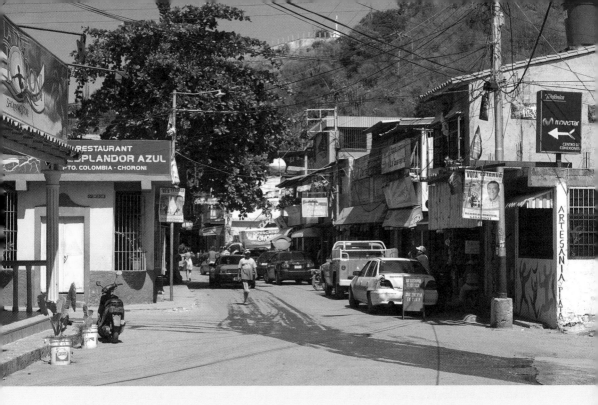

– with all eyes fixed on you as you made your way down the main street.

Choroni was much more cosmopolitan. There was music everywhere downtown, from reggae and salsa blasting out from the fruit stalls, to the famous tambores, or drum dancing, which took place on Saturday nights down by the sea wall promenade, next to the statue of St John the Baptist.

Weekend visitors still flock to watch as the drummers beat out complex rhythms on their huge cumaco drums, which are made from hollowed-out avocado tree trunks. It's a real spectacle: a singer steps forward to lead a call and response; a couple begins to dance; a circle of people forms around them; other dancers cut in to dance with either the man or the woman, gyrating wildly in the hot night air. It's thrilling stuff, and the party atmosphere it creates always lights up the rest of the town. We didn't find anything else quite like it on our travels.

One place we did love was Mochima National Park, along the north-east Caribbean coastline. It's a mountainous area and astoundingly beautiful, although very dry and arid in places. At the end of the day the temperature always fell sharply and suddenly, taking us by surprise.

With its warm, clear waters full of tropical fish, Mochima seemed like the ideal place to take our diving test, so we signed up for a course at a small school on the beach with a guy called Bluey, an American diving instructor.

One afternoon, just after we'd come out of the sea, I said, 'Shall I catch

Above: Puerto Colombia

supper?'

Little did Tania and Bluey know that I'd just spotted a monster flatfish basking in the shallows… quick as a flash, I ripped a branch off a palm tree, sharpened it with my penknife, waded back into the sea and skewered the fish with my makeshift spear.

'Here's supper!' I roared, raising it into the air. It was simply huge.

'That's my man!' Tania laughed when she saw the look of astonishment on Bluey's face.

That evening we built a barbecue on the beach. I salted the fish and grilled it on a rack over the open fire, then served it up with a local green sauce called *guasacaca*, which is a bit like guacamole. (It's made with onion, tomato, avocado, green peppers, coriander, salt and olive oil.)

The more Tania and I travelled, the more we were struck by all the different food specialities in Venezuela, which varied hugely from region to region. Setting out from the farm, we came across an area famous for its dairy products, including *suero de leche*, which is a tangy yogurt, and *suero de mantequilla* or *mantega*, which is a rich smooth buttermilk. Both are great breakfast treats.

The next zone was known for its delicious round soft white cheeses, which came in all kinds of subtle variations of flavour and texture. I particularly liked *queso guayanés*, which had rich, creamy flavour notes and was incredibly more-ish. Moving on, we sampled *casabi*, which are big, flat toasted discs made from yucca. You could put anything on *casabi* – sweet or savoury – and they tasted good. At the beach, we ate nothing but fish, on the seafront, every night. Then, away from the coast in the interior of the country, we discovered a wonderful roadside café that offered *chivo guisado*, a deliciously tender goat casserole. We were constantly sampling new dishes and flavours.

Back in Caracas, at the end of our travels, we both agreed that Venezuela felt like home. We loved the people, the food and all the different regions and landscapes. So then, was Choroni really where we wanted to be? We didn't even have to say it: of course it was. Mochima came close and we had a great time there, but it didn't have the lush green mountains dropping down to the sea, like Choroni; it didn't have the music, the dancing or the weekend life. The rest of Venezuela was there to be explored again and again, but we were making the right decision. It was time to visit Fernando Perreira again and put in an offer on the farm.

Right: Fruiting cacao trees

Chapter 2

I Become a Cacao Farmer

The origins of my chocolate journey go back several thousand years to when the ancestors of the Maya people began to cultivate cacao in the northern Amazon basin. They learned to ferment, roast and grind the cacao seeds into a paste, which they mixed with chilli, spices and cornmeal to make a frothy, bitter drink. It sounds unpalatable – revolting, even – but it was a fantastic pick-me-up energy booster and they couldn't get enough of it.

Cacao was highly prized throughout ancient Mesoamerica. It was known to fight tiredness, and people believed that it also cured stomach upsets and warded off colds and flu. The beans were used as currency, sometimes to pay taxes, and the drink was served at royal celebrations and used as a sacred libation to the gods. The Aztecs drank a similar concoction called *xocoatl* or *xocolatl*, which they associated with Xochiquetzal, the Maya goddess of fertility; they believed it to be an aphrodisiac. One Aztec king declared that *xocolatl* was 'a gift of paradise'.

Christopher Columbus was the first recorded European to come into contact with cacao. He took some beans back to the Spanish court, but their bitter taste didn't catch on with Ferdinand and Isabella. Later, when the Spanish conquered the Aztecs, cacao was one of the spoils of war. Once again, no one was too keen on the taste, but Hernándo Cortés, who conquered Mexico in 1521, issued *xocolatl* to his entire army. He claimed that just one cup gave each of his soldiers the strength and stamina to march all day.

Cacao soon made its way to Europe, where the Spanish heated up their *xocolatl*, adding milk and honey to combat the bitterness and replacing the chilli and spices with vanilla or cinnamon. They also invented a wooden stirring stick, a *molinillo*, that was used to whip the chocolate liquid into a smooth foam.

For a long time, Spain had a monopoly on cacao importation and chocolate was hugely expensive, the preserve of aristocrats and the Catholic Church. It was recognised for its restorative powers and used widely by fasting priests as a nutritional substitute for solid foods. Not only was it rich in vitamins and minerals, it was a powerful antioxidant and contained the stimulant theobromine, which kept everyone alert during vespers. (Theobromine is cacao's version of caffeine.)

During the seventeenth century, the craze for chocolate swept Europe. Subsequently, hundreds of thousands of indigenous people were enslaved to cultivate cacao on plantations throughout South America. The first chocolate house opened in London in 1657; thirty years later the physician Sir Hans Sloane developed a medicinal milk-and-chocolate drink in Jamaica, which was later sold to the Cadbury brothers.

Right: Ripe cacao pod

Chocolate production made leaps and bounds during the industrial revolution. Food pioneers experimented with extracting the fat from cocoa beans to make cocoa butter; they also tried to turn it into powder and remove the bitter taste by treating it with heat or alkali. One of them was Dutchman Conrad Van Houten, who in 1828 built a hydraulic press that separated cocoa butter from cocoa liquor and left cocoa powder, which he treated with alkali, a process that came to be known as 'Dutching'.

In 1847, Joseph Fry made the first solid chocolate for eating. More than thirty years later, in Switzerland, Daniel Peter successfully launched a milk chocolate bar – with the help of his neighbour, Henri Nestlé, who had developed a way to dehydrate milk and prevent mildew. Then Rodolphe Lindt invented the process called 'conching', which involves heating and grinding the cocoa solids to make them smoother and more integrated. Legend has it that Lindt discovered conching by accident, when one of his employees left a machine running all night. Chocolate as we know it had finally arrived.

Now that it was available to a much wider public, packed with powdered milk, sugar and other additives, chocolate began to lose its association with nutrition and energy. Instead it became a luxury product, and from there it developed into an indulgence: nice, but naughty and fattening.

I suppose that's how I also saw it, until I became a cacao farmer. But gradually I began to realise that, sometime during our love affair with sweet confectionery, we had lost touch with the amazing flavours and properties of real chocolate. Not only is it a wonder drug, it's a fantastic, versatile cooking ingredient, a powerful enricher of both sweet and savoury dishes – and I'd been missing out on it my whole life! Cacao fascinated me from the start, but little did I know that it was set to become a major obsession.

After Fernando agreed to sell us the farm, we expected to complete the deal fairly quickly. However, it wasn't that easy because Fernando's wife kept changing her mind about selling. He would call and say, 'I want to sell the farm today. Come with a lawyer!' So we'd arrive at his house, only for him to answer the door and say, 'My wife doesn't want to sell today. Come back next week.'

As a result of all this to-ing and fro-ing, Tania and I ended up camping on two nearby beaches, Cepe and Cuyagua, while we waited for the sale to be agreed. It was an amazing time, six months in total. There was so much to explore; each morning at the crack of dawn we went looking for a different lagoon to clean our teeth in.

We spent our days hunting, gathering and cooking: we fished together and cooked our catch over the campfire. We often saw the fishing boats come in to shore very early in the day. The fisherman had this beautiful tradition of laying out surplus fish for the people in the mountains when they'd had a very good catch, and then they'd sell the rest back in town. It was all part of the local community spirit.

When I went out fishing at night and reeled in a good catch, I used to lay my extra fish at the end of the rows of surplus. Gradually we got to know the fishermen and, as the months went by, one particular guy called Armado would say, 'Hey, Will, did you catch anything today?' And if I hadn't, he'd say, 'Take a fish!'

When we tired of eating fish, we'd walk up the slope behind the beach looking for a change of diet. On the way to Cepe village, there was a woman who kept livestock and one day we bought a chicken from her. After I'd killed it and plucked it, I looked at its scrawny legs and said to Tania, 'Now that's a real chicken!' Talk about a roadrunner! We went back to fish after that.

When we weren't catching supper, we swam and snorkelled or lay in our hammocks, head to head, playing backgammon. In the evenings, crabs would come along and try and nick the backgammon pieces: great big land crabs that

nip like mad with their one claw.

There was a beautiful set of cascading waterfalls behind Cepe beach, with one waterfall spilling into another. One of the pools was big enough so that you could leap right into the middle of it from a rock thirty feet above it. A glorious and refreshing way to wake up in the morning!

It was an idyllic life, but it couldn't go on forever. After nearly two years of waiting – of living on the beach and renting little houses in various villages – we still hadn't managed to buy the farm. Eventually we lost heart and went back to England. It was incredibly disappointing.

In London, I reluctantly resigned myself to city life. The plan was to sell my flat, buy a dilapidated house, do it up and go down the housing development route. My heart wasn't in it though. I was still dreaming of the farm, the shade canopies and the cacao.

A year passed. One night the phone rang. It was Fernando. 'Perreira here,' he said. 'Remember I always said I'd sell the farm to you? Well, the moment has finally arrived.'

I was still so passionate about the idea of the farm that I jumped at his offer. But Tania felt sceptical. She was worried that Fernando or his wife would change their minds again. I couldn't let it go, though, so we went to the Venezuelan Embassy to do some legal checks. As I was going up in the lift, discussing 'the farm in Choroni' with the secretary, a girl got in on the second floor and overheard us talking.

'What's the name of the farm?' she asked.

I turned to look at her and something – some instinct – told me that she was the daughter of the owner of the neighbouring five farms in Choroni. Rumbled!

'You're my neighbour's daughter,' I said. She looked absolutely astonished. 'It doesn't matter what the farm's called, because your father wants to buy it,' I added, attempting a nonchalant smile. Coincidentally, I'd heard that someone else was hoping to buy the farm from Fernando, so it wouldn't have surprised me to learn that his neighbour wanted it too.

'Oh, my father wants to buy the whole valley,' she said.

Tania and I realised that she would immediately call her father and tell him about our visit to the embassy. So we were going to have to move fast if we really wanted the farm, or we might lose it to rival buyers. First, I needed Tania's reassurance that this was what she really wanted. 'Go and try,' she said. 'If you get it, I'm with you all the way.' I flew to Venezuela the next day.

I landed on a Friday, began negotiating to buy the farm on the Monday and owned it by the following Friday, before anyone else had a chance to realise what had happened. 'I did it!' I screamed down the phone to Tania that night. 'We're moving to El Tesoro!'

A couple of months later, I flew on ahead to Venezuela, leaving Tania to tie up loose ends and finish saying goodbye to her family in England. I think she was hoping that before she arrived I would clear the paths around the hacienda of snakes and other nasty creatures.

On my first night at the farm, I took a chair out to the cacao-drying patio and sat down to drink a cuba libre, just as it was getting dark. I was all alone, absolutely *solito*; there was no one else for miles around. Right then an owl glided down into the canopies above the cacao.

It turned out that every night, at exactly twenty-to-seven, this owl took the same flight path past the same tree down into the cacao canopies. It was one of the most beautiful things ever. I took a swig of my drink and sighed contentedly. I had joined the flora and fauna of Venezuela.

I spent my first few days before Tania arrived roaming the land and exploring the farm, from the plantation down below to the very top of the cloud-forested mountain. Some areas felt like virgin territory and I had a strong sense that I was the first person to tread there. In other places there were sure signs of the hacienda's colonial past, when sugar cane had grown all the way up the sides of the mountain.

The farm was founded in 1640 as a cacao plantation and went on to grow sugar and coffee. It was also a distillery that produced the first stage of rum, a 35–40 per cent proof alcohol known as *aguardiente* or *caña clara*, sold under the El Tesoro label. Legend has it that smugglers used to bring bootleg liquor along the coast and up the road to the farm. Then the El Tesoro label would be slapped on it before it went over the mountain to be sold as legal liquor.

As I walked the land, I came across overgrown areas that had once been cleared for sugar processing; I also found broken copper bowls that had been used to heat up the sugar cane liquid. There were old stone walls and tumble-down houses roofed with beautiful Spanish-style tiles that had been made in kilns on the farm – remnants of another age that reeked of colonial nostalgia. At times I half expected a horse to come galloping around the corner, its rider dressed in a Spanish doublet and hose.

Everywhere you looked there was something growing, from

nutmeg trees on the farmhouse lawn to three-kilo avocados. There were seventy mango trees banked up against the side of the main house and in the mango season you could hear fruit falling all day and all night long: bong, bong, bang, bang. We estimated once that we had around thirty tons of mangoes. Fully-grown, the trees were ten metres high, and they produced every imaginable type of fruit, from the giant two-kilo manga to the piña, a type of mango that tasted slightly of pineapple.

We had Creole avocados, which were the original pre-hybrid avocados: they bruise easily, ripen quickly and have a smooth, buttery texture. The fruit of each avocado tree has a different flavour and I soon learned where my favourites were, dotted around the farm. We had guavas and guavitas, guyabanas (also known as soursops), oranges, mandarins, lemons, limon dulce (big sweet lemons), pepipan and namipalo (of the breadfruit family) and a huge, football-sized fruit called castaña, which was filled with South American chestnuts. There was also a cashew nut that was locally referred to as the 'devil's fruit' because the seed grew on the outside. The fruit was astringent and the juice dried your mouth when you bit into it.

There were guyavita: the size of peas, but so delicious and tender! There were little apple-pear type fruits called perita. One of my favourite plants was the pulmagar, which flowered just outside the house and carpeted the ground in brilliant pink when its stamens dropped; two months later it produced a big, red, luscious, succulent fruit that we used to make jam. Then there was the pulmerosa, a little yellow fruit. All sorts of animals found the pulmerosa irresistible and would sneak along to eat it, including lapa (large rabbit-type animals with short ears and big red eyes), ocuri (giant guinea pigs) and armadillos.

Best of all, we had cacao, more than twelve glorious hectares of it. It was something really special, too. 85 per cent of the world's cacao is made up of the Forestera strain of cacao; the other 15 per cent is comprised of the less bitter Criollo (Creole), Trinitario, Porcelana and variations of, which produce the beans with the interesting flavours. Our cacao was predominantly of Criollo characteristic, the best in the world; we also had a small amount of flavour-rich Trinitario. The principal crop came in November after the rainy season and there was another crop in July.

Although parts of the plantation had been neglected, in the main areas there were thousands of cacao trees growing in the shade of the tropical cloud forest, fed by nutrients and water passed down from the canopy above. Cacao must have shade to grow and our trees stood beneath twenty-metre tall African Mijao trees, which thrived along with them on the deep, moist, compost-rich soil

of the forest floor. Ginger plants prospered naturally beneath the cacao trees, shaded by their smooth, bright green oblong leaves.

Admittedly, the land required cleaning, the trees needed pruning and I was going to have to open up old irrigation channels to revive some of the shade trees, but that was fine with me. I relished the idea of hard work; I couldn't wait to get going.

We were lucky to have a great bunch of workers. Bertillio Araujo was a native of Choroni and had worked at El Tesoro for decades. He had a deep connection with the land and the plants and animals that inhabited it; I always looked to him for advice about growing, cultivating and harvesting. Ricardo Soto, Bertillio's nephew and quite a bit younger, was loyal, hardworking and quick to learn. The three of us worked very well together.

Since Tania and I had lived in the area for two years before we bought the farm, we already knew a lot of people and had started to build up good relationships. I've always thought it was difficult for people who go off to live abroad, whether in France, or Spain, or South America. You can get disheartened when you feel you don't fit in or aren't accepted locally, because it takes years to get a proper rapport going with people, the kind of relationship where you eat in each other's houses. It's a long-term thing.

Tania and I had lived on the beach for months. We'd also rented a little house downtown and spent time in other villages, so we knew people throughout the community. Some of the locals were probably quite surprised when we bought the hacienda, because we didn't act like the kind of people who could afford to buy a big farm. But by then we had already established strong ties and relationships, so it didn't matter. Our friendships had been established on an equal basis and were based on liking and trust, rather than status or possessions.

When Tania arrived, I picked her up at Caracas airport with a surprise in the back of the car. Two surprises, in fact: a couple of tiny, gorgeous, eight-week old Neapolitan mastiff puppies. They came from two different breeders and weren't related, so unfortunately they fought fiercely all through their first night together. Tania and I didn't sleep a wink either: it was torture listening to their constant scrapping and howling. Thankfully, by morning the fighting had stopped and after that they were the best of friends.

And so began the golden years of living at Hacienda El Tesoro. Tania and I were wildly happy; there was so much to explore and enjoy. It wasn't long before we made a start on restoring the various buildings, with a view to opening an eco-hotel. The National Park rules stated that you could only build on to existing buildings – or foundations – but that didn't appear to be a problem. We were in possession of the largest private complex of houses in the park and had the right to enlarge and modernise every one of the buildings, including the chicken sheds and pig houses that Fernando had added. There were fantastic possibilities for tourism. All we needed were a few official permissions.

Fernando had 'modernised' the main house, stripping it down and building it back with materials that didn't require much maintenance. This was understandable, because it was only his holiday home, but the result wasn't great aesthetically. We painted it and cleaned it out, and Tania added her 'tocacito' of style: there wasn't a lot more we could do unless we demolished and rebuilt it.

I installed underground electricity and water pipes throughout the farm complex. Then I did up the little building next to the main house, transforming it into a small, self-contained holiday house, which Tania decorated simply and beautifully. At that point, we began to get caught up in a spiral of bureaucracy: we were told that before we could go any further, full architectural plans had to be drawn up.

We were prepared to wait – or so we thought. Perhaps things would have been different if we had known in advance just how long it would take for the planning permissions to come through, but at the time we were blissfully ignorant of the way things worked. We had no idea how much red tape would be involved in the process.

In the meantime, I was happy to turn my full attention to the farm; I loved working with the guys. I made plans of the entire hacienda and divided it up into numbered zones (zona). That way we could say, 'Okay, let's work in zone 1 or 2 today,' and everybody knew what we were talking about.

We set about cleaning and clearing the land, pruning the cacao trees and opening up waterways to irrigate them. We'd start at 7am and stop for breakfast at about 10.30am, when either Ricardo's wife Annabel would bring arepas to the field, or Tania would call us up to the farmhouse. After breakfast, we went back to work until 3pm, when we knocked off for the day. The work was hot and sweaty, great physical exercise, and all the while I was busy learning about the hacienda. At 3pm I had lunch, or a rest, joined Tania at the beach or went downtown to get some fish for supper...

There were some small stores in Choroni village below us, but they really didn't have proper supplies, especially when we first arrived. So every week we had to drive an hour and a half to hot, dusty Maracay, especially if we

wanted anything from the hardware shop or supermarket. Trips to Maracay always consumed a lot of time. Just going to the shops and back would take up most of a day.

Other days we went high up into the mountains to collect bananas in the old colonial areas, taking Ricardo's and Bertillio's mules with us. I vividly remember cutting my first banana tree. Bertillio showed me how to gently chop the base and let it drop slowly until it bent over with the weight of the big cluster – or racimo – of bananas. Once it had flowered, fruited and matured, the tree was no longer viable, so you'd cut it down, take the bananas and the whole process would start all over again.

There were lots of different types of banana: titiaro, tepocco, mansano, cullaco, pineo, morada and many more. Each of them was great for something: the morada leaf was perfect for wrapping food and cooking it; tepocco were fantastic for making *tostones* (fried, flattened plantains); and mansano were deliciously small and sweet, with a slight apple flavour. There were always great big racimos of bananas at the back of the farmhouse, just in case anyone felt peckish. There wasn't much of a market for selling them, but they were good for eating, bartering for fish and feeding to the pigs.

Although we wrapped the bananas in leaves and carried them back in sacks, I learned never to wear clothes that I wanted to be seen in again when I went banana collecting, because the juice left permanent stains. Now I knew what those brown patches were on the local farmers' trousers!

Up and over the top of the mountain, which the locals called 'El Commandante', there was a small group of houses in a place known as Cambalache, which basically means 'exchange'. Directly above Chuao, the famous cacao hacienda, it was originally where people used to meet to barter and exchange goods; now it's a collection of smallholdings.

Every now and then we took the pack animals and spent the night at Cambalache. This was where the big cats roamed. I also spotted dantes – tapirs,

strange-looking animals with snouts and hooves – but it was rare to see the 200-kilo mountain leopards, fortunately. Sometimes we came across their paw prints just after it had rained, though, when the indentations of their toes and massive claws would be scarily well-defined. A bunch of old Cambalache guys used to sit around reminiscing about the days when they hunted and shot big cats. They reminded me a bit of fishermen with their tall stories.

There were signs of animals all over the farm, but we were in a national park and I quickly made it known that the new owner didn't hunt or eat the wildlife. If I wanted to hunt, I went fishing on the beach or caught crayfish in the river. The crayfish – or camarones – were black, with huge great claws; some of them grew to half a kilo. You could find them under the stones in the river and catch them by hand, just by feeling along the edges of a large rock until your two hands met.

If there was a crayfish under there, its antennae would touch your fingers and it would react by moving away in the other direction – only to be caught in the middle when your hands came together. It was the creepiest thing to feel its spidery tickle underwater and I was pinched many times – but it was worth it when you lifted an almighty camaron from under the rock!

Camaron fishing was best at night, in the dark, when you fished them with a small hook and a very fine line. It was incredibly fun and exciting. Ricardo loved it because it took him back to his boyhood adventures. You'd see insects you'd never seen before and all kinds of animals. One night I was down by the stream with some friends, when I heard a splash behind me. Assuming it was one of the guys messing around, I quickly flipped my flashlight around. There, just six feet away from me, frozen in the beam of my torch, I saw a lapa, a beautiful giant rabbit type of animal. 'Look!' I called to the guys. Afterwards, it was the talk of the farm. Even the Venezuelans said they had never been that close to a lapa.

Of course, some of the animals we encountered weren't quite so benign.

Since the house hadn't been properly lived in for years, we were constantly coming across snakes. One afternoon in the very early days at the farm, I was collecting oranges by the river, using a pole to knock them off the trees. As I reached down to pick up an orange, I noticed an enormous coiled macao, stirring slightly, just half a metre away from my hand. My God! I thought. My heart started pounding.

I edged backwards and, using the pole, I lunged at the snake, catching it half way down its body. Pinned to the spot, it began thrusting out at me, hissing wildly. I shouted for Bertillio, who rushed to the rescue. With a flash of his machete, he quickly chopped off its head; he was incredibly skilled at wielding a machete.

Another time, I was walking in the forest when a snake lunged at my head from the path above me. The image of its face so close to mine remains utterly clear and vivid in my mind to this day. Its gums were pulled back and its eyes bulging. It was the scariest sight! Thankfully it didn't reach me, but it dropped to the ground beside me. I didn't wait around to see what would happen next: I legged it.

There was a huge amount of local superstition surrounding snakes. For centuries, being bitten by a snake had meant almost certain death, and only recently had the locals been able to get their hands on an accessible antidote. Everybody had a family member who had died from a snakebite. So if you saw a snake, you killed it – otherwise it would kill you.

People were a little bit more understanding about the boas, known as trago de venau. Years later, a boa constrictor lived in a hole right in the middle of our vegetable garden, which people seemed to find rather quirky.

Spiders were another type of creature I wasn't particularly fond of. One day I was in the bathroom – a couple of months after we first moved in – when I looked down to my left and saw the mother of all black tarantulas a few inches from my foot. I'd obviously disturbed her: she was raising a couple of her hairy legs in rather a threatening way.

I didn't scream, but I quickly moved away and thought, Phew, blimey! Outside the bathroom, I pulled my pants up, found a broom and gently took her outside. The next day, in the bathroom again, I looked down to where she had been – and there she was again! This time I took her outside and I killed her, because that was obviously where she lived and I didn't want to meet her again.

It was only later that I realised that tarantulas could be house spiders; they were attracted by the light and were everywhere in the house. Their bite wasn't so bad, but there was always the danger that they would spray venomous stuff at you, or their fine hairs would get stuck in you. I had huge admiration for Ricardo because he allowed them to walk all over his body, but I kept my distance.

A tarantula never got me, but I did step on something nasty when I was walking in the mountains with Ricardo and my friend William Alldous, also known as Willcito. Suddenly I saw a cloud of yellow and black rising up towards me. Whoa, I thought, wasps! I instantly threw down my machete and started running away, covering my face with my hands. 'Ricardo, ayuda mi!' I shouted as they swarmed around my head and went on to sting every exposed inch of skin on my body.

Fifty metres away, Ricardo and Willcito were astonished to see me running through the jungle like a loony, waving my arms around and screaming. What's Willie up to? they wondered, oblivious to my agony.

By the time they realised what was going on, I had been stung at least sixty times. 'What can we do?' they said repeatedly. I simply roared like an Araguata monkey. Something told me that I could get rid of the poison if I made a lot of noise.

I was fortunate that I hadn't stumbled on the worst type of wasps in the jungle, and even more fortunate that I'm not allergic to wasps. But I never found that machete again and it became a point of reference on the farm, known evermore as 'the place where I lost that machete'.

I was always conscious of the fact that I was surrounded by the most incredible biodiversity. Often it felt as if I was living in a David Attenborough film. It was commonplace to sit on a wall and see a little wasp lying on the ground below me. It was like a dance: the wasp pretended to be injured; a spider came along to eat it; the wasp surprised the spider and stung it, then circled it while the venom slowly paralysed it; finally the wasp dragged the spider away, immobilised but still alive, and laid its eggs inside its body.

Every time I saw this happen, or heard the chatter and whoops of the monkeys in the trees, or caught the rainbow flash of the stripes down the side of a male armadillo, or spotted a toucan or a sloth or an anteater, I was reminded of how privileged I was to be living at El Tesoro.

I couldn't wait for the first cacao harvest in November, even though harvesting is a lot of work. There are so many stages: picking the pods, carrying them to a collection point, opening them up, scraping the seeds on to a plastic sheet, lugging them in a bucket back up to the hacienda, putting them in fermentation boxes and stirring them twice a day, then laying them out on the

Right: Processing the cacao pods – the opening

patio and turning them all day long. It was incredible to see how many factors were involved in evolving the cacao bean to its finished state, to reach the quality you're after. It's not like picking apples or harvesting grain. It's a long, labour-intensive process!

When the pods had reached their absolute peak of ripeness, Bertillio showed me how to cut them down using a machete, taking care not to damage the budding new flowers. Next came the fermenting process, which helps to remove acidity. It's also the stage where the beans develop their distinctive aroma and flavour, so it is crucial to get it right.

Inside the pod, the beans are coated in a slippery, white, sweet pulp; it's delicious, but it tastes nothing like chocolate. We placed the beans in hardwood boxes covered with banana leaves and left them for three days while the white pulp fermented, turning them twice a day to aerate them. I was amazed to learn that the temperature inside the boxes reaches over 50 degrees.

Next, we laid the beans out on the cacao patios of the hacienda and turned them constantly as they gently dried in the sun. Everything was done properly, without cutting corners, so for the first couple of days we didn't dry them in the full tropical glare – just in the morning and in the evening for a few hours. Then we slowly increased their sun exposure until they were done, which took about a week. The way you make sure they're completely dry is to weigh them, put them out in the sun and weigh them again afterwards. If there's no weight loss, they're done.

Now there is something very satisfying about harvest time. And even more so when you're following your dream on your own farm and you're harvesting your own crop for the very first time. I can still remember my first beans. They were a beautiful golden-red-brown colour. I stood on the patio and rolled them in the palm of my hand, mesmerised by the way they shone in the sunlight.

An incredible feeling of excitement came over me. I had become a cacao farmer! I was on my way to making my own chocolate. After all that travelling, and all that waiting, I had finally found the life I'd been searching for.

Chapter 3

Chocolate is a Drug...

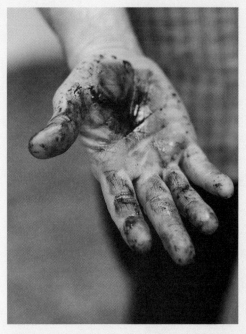

Bertillio and Ricardo taught me the rudiments of cacao-making in the kitchen at the back of the farmhouse. I was amazed by the methodology: the roasting takes the flavour to another level, and the shelling produces cacao nibs, the edible part of the bean. The nibs then go through a grinder that crushes and aerates them to release the cacao butter. (Approximately 50 per cent of each nib is cacao butter.) The transformation of the beans into a beautiful chocolate elixir struck me as quite miraculous. I was hooked.

Once I understood the basic process, I began to finesse it. I was meticulous at every stage. The key was not to over-roast the beans, so I pan-roasted them for between fifteen and twenty minutes per batch, depending on the moisture content, using a big cast-iron pan and a timer. When one batch was done, the next lot immediately went in with a clatter and ping. It was like clockwork, steady and continuous. I learned that you've got to have continuity to get consistent results.

There was lots of trial and error. At first I shelled the beans by hand, before I worked out how to gently break them with a flat stone. Then I dropped them in front of a small fan tilted at about 45 degrees so that the husk blew away and I was left with the nibs.

I ground the nibs using a small electric grinder. Then I ground them again, and again. Finally I worked out that they needed to be put through the grinder at least five times to reach the smoothness I was looking for.

I hadn't realised how much work goes into making chocolate, from bean to bar. It's quite incredible. I can't think of another raw material that goes through so many stages of processing. But, as with the harvest, it was pointless trying to take short cuts. Making cacao was labour-intensive and there was no getting around it.

I didn't mind how long it took. The whole procedure thrilled me. Of course it did: I was, after all, just a grown-up version of the twelve-year-old who had become totally absorbed in the complex process of winemaking in Ireland. And without having made cacao so painstakingly, by hand, I don't think I would have understood so well how to make it on a larger scale.

The cacao liquor I produced was a revelation, characterised by rich, fruity, rounded notes, with zing! I had no idea that chocolate could taste so good. Hang on a second, I thought, the possibilities are huge!

The very first thing I made with my cacao was a hot chocolate drink. It seemed the obvious choice to follow in the footsteps of the Mayans and Aztecs by drinking a fabled cup of *xocolatl*, albeit in a less bitter, less spicy, far more palatable form. So I mixed cacao liquor with water and honey and heated it up in a saucepan. The first rich, chocolaty mouthful blew my mind. 'Tania, come here! You've got to taste this,' I shouted. 'It's incredible!'

Almost immediately after I had drunk that first cup, I was struck by a physical feeling of energy and wellbeing. Tania experienced it too. She suggested a walk up the mountain to see the howler monkeys, even though it was the middle of the day, and soon we found ourselves marching energetically up through the cloud forest, fuelled by a dynamic surge of power.

Suddenly we realised that what is known as chocolate in England is actually a distant cousin of the real thing, and that true chocolate is in fact a drug. No wonder it was revered by the Mayans and Aztecs! Hot chocolate soon became the welcome drink of El Tesoro.

'What's next?' Tania asked, as we made our way down the mountain.

'It's got to be Chocolate Nemesis!' I said. 'Yee-ha!'

We both loved the famous River Café recipe, which has to be one of the most intense chocolate puddings in the world. And although the Nemesis I made was an adaptation of the original recipe, using sugar, butter, eggs and cacao, it turned out to be the perfect way to taste the cacao's flavour notes.

As we spooned this deeply rich, dark and delectable piece of heaven into our mouths, Tania's eyelashes fluttered with pleasure. The taste

sensation was overwhelming. I had never sampled anything as gorgeously delicious in my entire life.

'Unbelievable! Incredible!' we kept saying. 'Made from our very own cacao beans!' It was a truly momentous occasion. In fact, that first Nemesis almost felt like an offering to the gods, which was fitting, because we had a lot to be thankful for.

Inevitably I started to think about making my own chocolate, especially as I couldn't help but notice that the cacao bars being made locally were very poor quality. The guys producing cacao downtown didn't bother shelling the beans; they just ground up the shells and threw them in the mix, or roasted everything in a pot and added maize to make the liquor go further. I knew I could do better.

A piece of piping was my accidental hero. I couldn't think of what to use as a mould and wandered into my workshop, racking my brain for an answer. Suddenly I noticed a long length of plastic pipe on the floor. Aha! I chopped it up, sanded and sterilised it to make hundreds of cylindrical moulds. As it happened, it turned out to be the perfect shape for a cacao bar: it's great for grating and keeps better because it's got less surface area than flat bars. It also went on to distinguish me from other chocolate-makers.

I laid out hundreds of the pipe sections on metal trays; then Ricardo, Tania and I got to work. The kitchen at the hacienda exploded with the delicious, heady smell of chocolate as we roasted, shelled and ground kilo upon kilo of cacao. Everybody in Choroni knew what we were up to because the aroma wafted down the valley into the town. Bertillio could even smell it from his house across the valley: he'd always come to lend a hand, if he wasn't at the farm.

The cacao liquor became very warm when it went through the grinder, so it was easy to pour into the moulds. Next we rushed it to the freezer to remove the heat quickly. This was a very crude way of tempering the chocolate, of heating and cooling it to ensure that the solids and the cacao butter don't separate.

A few hours later, we took the moulds out of the freezer, removed the bars, put a cloth over them to prevent condensation and immediately wrapped them in foil.

We quickly became known locally for our delicious 100 per cent cacao bar. We sold it at the market downtown and through the guesthouses and posadas. People couldn't get enough of it. I soon realised that I could generate more income producing bars of cacao than simply selling the crop as beans, especially later when my great friend and cacao buyer John Kehoe left the country and I was left to the mercy of the local buyers. It meant a lot of hard work,

though: the principal crop was about 600 kilos when we first took over the farm.

Tania and I went on experimenting with cacao in the kitchen, producing endless chocolate delights. We made ice cream, sauces and cakes, and mixed cacao with chilli to make rich coulis. Since I couldn't get hold of real cream to make truffles, I improvised by reducing ripe mangoes and guyabanas, which I folded into the grated cacao to make delicious, naturally-sweet, fruit ganaches.

I tried my sauces and puddings out on everyone who came to the farm. Some people couldn't believe their tastebuds; as the rich, chocolaty flavour registered on their faces, their expressions would become incredulous. That's because the local cooking culture in Choroni, fantastic as it is, doesn't have much of a tradition of the kind of chocolate desserts that we go mad about in England. The desserts and puddings produced downtown are almost exclusively coconut-based.

Chocolate was becoming a huge passion in my life. Since the key to good cacao is good beans, I decided to improve and replant large areas of the plantation, at the same time expanding cacao production. One very large plain, which we called Zona 4, seemed like the perfect place to start replanting. Some

Above: First stage of harvesting – the collection

of the trees there had died because the waterways had been cut and the area hadn't been maintained for years.

Replanting that area turned out to be one of the most pleasurable experiences of my life, even though it was a big job clearing and cleaning the land in readiness for the new trees. I thought deep and hard about what kind of trees to replant and did my research into the different strains. Criollo seemed the obvious choice. The bean, when ripe, is white inside; it then dries light brown and without much acidity, rendering it perfect for chocolate-making because it doesn't need much sugar, which masks the flavours. Criollo also has a lovely, full, aromatic flavour. What's more, it just so happens to trace its ancestry to the birth of the Theobroma cacao species in the northern Amazon basin. It felt right in every way.

Since the farm had been around since 1640, I had a mixture of trees that had evolved through the centuries. My beans already had a Criollo characteristic, but the cacao tree cross-pollinates over the years, creating various hybrid fruits. I decided I wanted to keep the characteristic flavour of the beans on the farm, while at the same time improving it with other, purer Criollo strains.

Where would I find a purer Criollo strain? I called on my friend John Kehoe for some advice. He is one of the most knowledgeable people in the world when it comes to cacao, a real expert.

I already knew that I had a better chance of finding purer strains in

Venezuela than I would anywhere else in the cacao-growing world. Back in the 1950s, Venezuela produced over half the world's cacao, but the rise of oil and petroleum meant that traditional industries were neglected. As a result, the original strains of Venezuelan cacao have been left untampered with in the intervening years, whereas cacao growers in the rest of the world have been producing hybrid strains that yield bigger crops, at a cost to flavour and aroma.

When I told him about my plans, John Kehoe immediately began talking about a legendary farm in Costa Maya, where the trees were reputed to be pure, unadulterated Criollo. He knew about the farm because, once a year, a man would turn up at his offices to sell a few sacks of beans that had been grown and harvested there. The beans were the best, purest Criollo cacao he'd ever seen, he said! I pressed him for more information, but there was nothing he could add. All he knew was that the farm was at Costa Maya, a region that is famous for growing coffee. He didn't know who owned it or anything else about it.

It's a four to five-hour journey to Costa Maya from El Tesoro, even though it's probably only about 30 kilometres from Choroni as the crow flies, because the road takes you over the mountains to Maracay and then doubles back over the mountains to Costa Maya. A few days after speaking to John, I set off with Ricardo to find the mysterious hacienda and its fabled cacao, thinking it couldn't be too hard to locate.

My imagination was fired up. I had to see these amazing beans! But although we searched high and low throughout the region, the farm was nowhere to be found. No one local seemed to have heard of it, or if they had they couldn't pinpoint where it was. I started to wonder if it really existed. Frustrated and tired, we made our way back to El Tesoro with an empty truck.

I tried to put Costa Maya out of my mind and began researching other sources of Criollo beans. Then I heard some very interesting news on the Choroni grapevine: my neighbour had discovered the elusive plantation! What's more, one of his workers was willing to tell us where it was. Ricardo got the information out of him over a few beers, and we set off again, this time with precious directions.

It was little wonder the farm had been so difficult to find, because our route soon took us off the main road and we hit a network of dirt tracks that led into the middle of nowhere. A couple of times the track forked and Ricardo said, 'Hey, he didn't say anything about this!' so we had to take wild stabbing guesses about which way to go. 'Left!' Ricardo yelled at one point. Since the dirt track going left looked better maintained than the dirt track forking right, we went left.

Left: Ascent to Colonia Tovar from La Victoria

We went for miles and miles before coming to a dead end. Then we had to turn round, return to the fork in the road and try going right instead. This was a darker, far narrower road. At one point it was so steep that concrete plinths had been laid all along the centre of the track to provide a surface to grip on to during the descent. If it rains, I thought, we're never getting out of here! We still didn't know if we were even going in the right direction.

I was tempted to call it a day and head back, but John Kehoe's voice kept echoing around my head: 'It's the best cacao I've ever seen, the best cacao, the purest Criollo…' An image of the plain at Zona 4 rose into my mind's eye, the land cleared and ready to be replanted. I gripped the steering wheel and pressed my foot down on the accelerator. I had to go on. I couldn't give up.

Finally, at long last, we found the farm, at the end of the bumpiest, dustiest road I've ever driven down. We pulled up in front of a cluster of buildings that looked neatly kept and well-maintained. We'd been told to ask for someone called Felix at the hacienda, but a woman at the house said he was in the fields. So we loped off to find him and at last we met up with him on his way back from the nurseries, walking along with a couple of hacienda workers.

Felix was a lovely, chatty, gentle man in his fifties, who spoke impeccable English. He was very happy to help us. I think he enjoyed the opportunity to share all his knowledge. His constant flow of conversation reminded me of how I'd been when I was travelling around South America and hadn't spoken English for a while – he was full of energy!

Although Felix didn't actually own the hacienda, he had run it and managed it for years. He was very proud of the cacao and knew everything there was to know about it. He didn't have a fridge so we never ate together, but he made the most wonderful coffee. His unusual cooking techniques fascinated me. He drew on Pasteur's philosophy: he boiled his meat in a pan, ate his fill, replaced the lid and re-boiled it, being careful not to take the lid off. The next day, he would re-boil the pan, eat his fill, replace the lid and re-boil – and so on, for days on end. Eventually, of course, all the flavour was in the consommé. Unfortunately, the next time I visited, he had been gravely ill because someone had taken the lid off his pot of re-boiled meat without telling him.

Over a coffee, Felix told me that the hacienda was, and had always been, a coffee plantation, like all the haciendas in the region. But a hundred years ago, someone had come along and planted 1,200 cacao trees. Nobody knew why. It was just a random thing that the owner did.

There were two important reasons why these cacao trees were so special. Firstly, they hadn't cross-pollinated with other cacao trees, because there weren't any other cacao trees to be found in the region. So they really were pure Criollo! Secondly, they were growing in the same shade trees as the coffee, which happened to be bucari trees.

Felix explained that bucari roots provided highly nutritious nitrogen supplements to the soil, which might explain why these cacao trees were absolutely huge and produced lots of fruit. They were such outstanding specimens that scientists from a specialist chocolate company had come from France and numbered each tree according to its characteristics, grading it from one to fifteen according to its quality. This made things a lot easier for me. I took all my seeds from the best trees!

I was deliriously happy as I drove back to El Tesoro. I had empty pockets but a full truck; Felix had sold me 350 pods of the purest Criollo in the country.

Back at the hacienda, we opened the pods and meticulously cleaned the white pith off the seeds, then laid them on hessian sacks that we'd soaked in water and laid another sack on top of them. We left them in the bathrooms to germinate: the tiled walls and floors meant that they were the coolest rooms on the farm and less likely to dry out the seeds. I remember Tania threatening to go mad because every time she tried to go to the bathroom, it would be full of seeds germinating under sacks.

The seeds took three or four days to germinate. The air was thick with the smell of them exploding into life, and then out came little white shoots, about a quarter of a centimetre long. We'd already filled thousands of bags with a mixture of sand, mulch and tierra negra (black soil). We planted each seed with the sprout pointing downwards.

We potted around 7,000 seedlings in one go and tended them assiduously. All seemed to be working out smoothly – until one morning when Ricardo came to find me in my workshop. I immediately knew from his expression that something was wrong. He looked seriously worried.

'What is it?' I asked.

'The leaves are dropping off the plants,' he said.

My heart thumped in sudden panic. I couldn't lose all those thousands of plants! 'What's the problem?'

'I don't know!' he wailed.

No one knew. I followed him outside to inspect the viveros, the nurseries.

The stems of the little plants were green when you scratched them, which meant they were still living, but the leaves were dropping off in their hundreds. Oh my God! I thought. What are we going to do?

The next day things were worse. It was startling to see so many little plants without their leaves. It caused panic and mayhem among us. Ricardo was worried that he'd done something wrong. I wondered if there was a problem with the water, or something in the air. I turned every possibility over in my head as I tried to figure it out, but I couldn't come up with the cause – or a solution. Something unknown was killing the shoots and stopping the new leaves from forming.

We rushed down the mountain to ask 'Mucoso', my neighbour's farm manager, for advice. 'Is it in the nursery?' he asked. We nodded. 'You can relax, then,' he said with a smile. 'It sounds like a mild fungus to me. It can happen when you have a lot of small plants together and they get over-moist.'

I couldn't believe that such a big problem could be so simply resolved, but he was right. He suggested a friendly herbal spray, which got rid of the fungus in no time. It was the most incredible relief. There was no way I could have afforded to go back to Costa Maya and buy another ten thousand seeds.

When the plants reached 70–80cm after about six months, we planted them out on the plain, five metres one way and four metres the other, giving them lots of space. In other areas, I planted seeds that I selected from the existing trees on the hacienda, because I liked their distinct flavour. I didn't try to maximise my use of the ground. I took the view that an organic tree needs a certain amount of space to grow. A thousand trees per hectare seemed about right.

No pesticides, fertilisers or chemicals have ever been used on our cacao trees, which are irrigated by water that runs down from the cloud forest-topped mountains. The environment that cacao grows in is very fragile; very small insects pollinate the flowers, so it's not a place you introduce pesticides in any shape or form. There was also the fact that we were in a national park and the use of chemicals was forbidden.

So the trees were and remain totally organic, unofficially, at least. At one point a reputable organic association came to inspect us and the inspectors gave us a transition of a year to be fully licensed. But at the end of our transition we decided that we didn't need to pay anyone to tell us we were organic. You either are or you're not – it seems to me that the word has been hijacked for profit and put beyond the reach of small farmers.

While my passion for cacao grew, a steady stream of visitors began to flow through the farm. At first it was friends, then friends of friends; soon all kinds of

Left: Nursery at Hacienda San José

people had heard about what we were doing on the farm and wanted to come and meet us and explore. For the time being, until we got the eco-hotel off the ground, we were happy to offer something to suit everyone's budget. If people wanted cheap, they could rent a hammock on the farmhouse roof and wake up to the amazing jungle dawn. For a little bit more, they could sleep in a comfortable room, or take over the little house next to the main house.

I constantly took people on walks up the mountain or through the jungle. It was always an adventure, because you can't predict what nature will throw at you. Mostly it was a good adventure, but one day the adventure turned into a nightmare when I decided to take some friends for a swim in a big pool called Lejau, about a fifteen-minute walk from El Tesoro.

Surrounded by thick forest, with a waterfall you can slide down, Lejau is absolutely beautiful. I often went fishing there at the weekends. A wonderful feeling of tranquillity would always engulf me the moment it came into view. It reminded me of the enchanted pools you read about in fairytales as a child.

This particular day I took my friend John Paul, his wife Sophie and their kids, and a guy named Tom Vogel, whom we'd met at the beach the previous day. Sophie and the children stayed on the banks while John Paul, Tom and I crossed

the pool to just below the waterfall. As we were debating whether to climb up, it suddenly turned mud-brown and the flow became a torrent.

'Guys, it's a flash flood, quick!' I shouted. We jumped back into the pool like lemmings and tried to swim across it.

Within seconds, the water level had risen several metres and we were caught in a remolino, a whirlpool. Since I'm not a strong swimmer, I had stayed close to the edge, so I was the first one out. I hauled myself up on to the side.

John Paul, a better swimmer, had gone further, but not as far as Tom, who was a really strong swimmer. Tom was right in the thick of the whirlpool. So while John Paul managed to pull himself out on another side, Tom was struggling in the middle. He was thrashing around and kept going under.

Unfortunately, there was nothing we could do except shout out instructions until we were hoarse. 'Swim towards where the water comes into the pool!' we kept yelling. This would have seemed illogical to him because there was a huge roar of water coming from that area.

It was terrible to see his panic-stricken face as he fought to stay above the water; it almost felt worse that we hardly knew him. He managed to thrash out a couple of forward crawls in the right direction, but then he got caught in the flick of the whirlpool. He came round the swirl once and I grabbed out for him, but missed him by an inch. My heart began to pound; my mouth went dry. We had to get him out now or he was going to drown. He was seconds away from dying.

He came round again, desperately trying to make his way to the edge, while the current sucked him back and under. He made one last supreme effort to throw himself at the side and somehow, miraculously, he made it!

John Paul and I dragged him up out of the water and laid him on the ground. He was gasping for breath and so exhausted that he couldn't stand up. His legs were like jelly and he had to lie down for at least half an hour before he could even think about walking home. And so it was that we all bonded for life: ever since that day, we've been the greatest of friends. After an ordeal like that, how could you not be? We felt so incredibly glad to be alive.

We always joked afterwards about the time that 'we went down to the river to play, and no one came back!' I'm not sure Sophie saw the funny side, though. It was a horrific experience for her and the children to watch Daddy nearly die.

Funnily enough, every time I told the story, I mistakenly described the whirlpool, a 'remolino', as a 'remolacha', which means 'beetroot' – much to people's surprise. 'What? You say you got caught in a big beetroot?' By now I was a fluent Spanish speaker, but it was just one of those words I had a block about.

It turned out that Lejau was something of a death trap; around seventy people have died there over the years. I had heard that there was a cave you could get sucked into, but I was always under the impression that it was immediately beneath the rock face facing the slide. Years later I was told that in fact it was to the left at the bottom of the waterfall, and after that I was much more wary of going there.

Then one night I had a dream that I was going down the slide repetitively, and the very last time I went down I got sucked into the cave. Why, why, why did I go down that last time? I was thinking, in the dream. It's funny – Lejau is a dangerous place and I really should avoid it, yet I often daydream about fishing there, amid the beauty and tranquillity of the forest. Maybe it really is enchanted.

Back at the farm, Tania and I cooked up a storm in our kitchen, playing with all kinds of jungle ingredients, especially cacao. I stuck by the lessons I had learned as a boy in Ireland, in particular the idea that the best food can be very simple, as long as you use quality ingredients. I had been cooking trout, salmon, sea bass and mackerel practically all of my life, along with roasts and stews and spaghetti bolognese: I'd always been interested in cooking methods and food combinations.

We explored all kinds of cooking and offered up some really beautiful suppers and puddings. People started coming back just for the food, and I saw it as a challenge to invent a new chocolate recipe every time. We were constantly racking our brains to think of new ways to cook things, so that our repeat visitors wouldn't get bored. Seafood, sushi, moles, risottos, soups, truffles, cakes, biscuits – our repertoire of dishes expanded on a weekly basis.

It became increasingly clear to me that cacao was a powerful enricher. The more I cooked with it, the more I realised how versatile it was. I began adding it to all kinds of dishes, savoury and sweet. It was a natural progression to use it as a condiment, a flavour-enhancer, like salt.

I found it to be a remarkable addition to savoury cooking: it seemed to enrich almost everything, including meat casseroles, chicken arepas, curry, risotto and even gazpacho. It's our conditioning that makes us think that chocolate is purely sweet, when in actual fact it's the most wondrous ingredient, whether you use it for savoury or sweet. As with salt, adding just a little amount can strengthen and bring out the flavours of food, or simply add depth and richness and body. It's amazing. These days I couldn't be without cacao in the kitchen. It lives by the olive oil.

Fortunately, the young trees from Costa Maya flourished on the plain at

Right: Cooking cachapas by the roadside

Zona 4. Like all cacao trees, they would take between three to five years to mature and meanwhile they required a lot of tending and attention. It's very important to prune frequently and clean around the bases of the trees to keep the weeds away. Making sure that they're properly irrigated is also vital, obviously.

As the years passed, I began to gain a much better understanding of the different stages of cacao growing, harvesting and processing. I became quite scientific about the fermenting stage, making records of the size and appearance of the beans and the weather conditions every season.

At first Bertillio and Ricardo were fermenting the beans for three days and nights. Since over-fermentation can mean losing out on flavour, one year I tried shortening the time to two nights and three days to see what effect it had. Through trial and error, I learned to adjust the length of fermenting time, mainly judging it from the appearance of the fermented bean.

One season, I couldn't take the beans out of the fermentation boxes because it was raining. I noticed that the extra fermentation time meant that the bean went darker and had a very chocolaty flavour, but crucially it didn't have so many of the flavour notes that distinguished it from other cacao. It was tricky getting the right combination, because there are so many factors involved. However, the more I learned and experienced, the easier it became. Soon I was producing a consistently high-quality bean.

When I walked over the Zona 4 plain and inspected the trees, I always experienced a huge sense of pleasure at the thought that I had helped to nurture and plant them. The cacao they now produce is fantastic, with a beautiful Creole characteristic. As they say in Venezuela, 'Vale la pena.' (It's worth the trouble!) Replanting Zona 4 was my first significant step towards restoring the hacienda and putting it back on the map.

Chapter 4

Holding on to the Dream

Life was great. We were incredibly happy. Yet a strange feeling began to creep up on me as I hurtled towards my mid-thirties. I started wondering, Where am I going with all of this? What's it all for? Everything was fantastic... but something was missing.

Luckily, Tania had it all in hand. In 1998 we had our first child, Sophia, and there it was, that space was filled. Suddenly everything slotted into place. I realised what life was about and why we were doing all these things: for our kids.

I rang all my friends in England and told them to hurry up and have babies. 'It's the best thing ever! Children make the world go round,' I told them over and over again. It was as if I was the first person ever to have discovered the joy of having children – and that's how it felt: new and amazing and exciting.

Tania had Sophia by Caesarian section in a clinic in Maracay, an hour and a half away from the farm. I wasn't allowed into the operating theatre. The doctors cited hygiene as the reason, but I think it was more about different ideas and philosophies. I wasn't present at the birth of our second child, William, for the same reason two years later. It was only back in England when I witnessed the arrival of Evie, our third, that I realised what a huge deal having a Caesarian is. It was dramatic and momentous. It really made me wish I'd been at the births of Sophia and William.

We were thrilled when Sophia arrived. She was incredibly sweet and beautiful and I was full of protective love for her. But it was difficult for Tania to have her first baby in a foreign country, without her family nearby. It's usual to be surrounded by relatives, and you look to your mum or sister for help, reassurance and advice, especially with your first child. Having your family around makes you feel more secure. So although we had people to help out around the house, we missed our family and friends, especially as our phone was linked to a satellite and didn't work when there was too much cloud cover. Tania's family made frequent visits, which helped, but it wasn't the same.

Naturally, you feel anxious with your first baby, and we certainly did our fair share of worrying. Add to that a sense of isolation, the insecurity of being in the middle of nowhere and the fear of tropical disease and deadly insects... and it gets quite a lot more complicated. Of course, the flip side of this is that the tropics are a wondrous place for kids to grow up, because there's so much going on. But having children changed our priorities. All we cared about was their safety and wellbeing.

As Sophia – and then William – grew up, we had all the normal pitfalls of water and drowning and falling over, but also the added worries of snakes, spiders, scorpions, killer bees, poisonous centipedes, ants and other insects, none of which you have to worry about in England. We had to be constantly vigilant.

We were very conscious of rivers, because frogs are a staple diet of snakes, which is why snakes hang out by the riverbank. There is also a black and white stripy fly that is active in the morning and evening. It infects you with a parasite when it bites, transmitting leishminiasis.

When my sister Sophie and her boyfriend Charlie came to stay, Charlie was bitten by one of these flies, unbeknown to everyone. Months later I saw him in England and he said, 'I've got this sore from a bite that hasn't gone away. What do I do?'

I took one look at the hole in his leg and told him to get down to the School of Tropical Medicine! A few strong antibiotics later, the sore cleared up.

When you're living up a mountain in the middle of the jungle, you're a long way from everything, including doctors. Cleanliness and hygiene are ultra-important, as is eating well. But however careful you are, something's always going to get you.

Thankfully, Tania and the children managed to avoid major illnesses and accidents, apart from one terrible time when William fell down a flight of stairs, when he was a toddler. I, on the other hand, was not so lucky.

The first time I ended up in hospital happened to coincide with a visit from Tania's family. While she was off picking them up from the airport, I spent the day cutting tiles for the swimming pool. It was hot work on a hot day and I became dehydrated without realising it. Dehydration was something you really had to watch for in that climate. You had to drink water constantly, even when you didn't feel thirsty.

I had this crazy guy helping me to renovate a load of old furniture I'd picked up in Maracay; after I'd finished doing the tiles, he spent the rest of the afternoon telling me about aliens landing and the Martians coming. So I was very relieved when I heard the sound of the car: I leapt to my feet and ran right across the patio to greet Tania and her parents as they came up the drive. Unfortunately, because I was so dehydrated, standing up quickly gave me an almighty head rush. I fainted, fell off the edge of the patio, plunged about six feet and landed on the gravel right in front of the car, smashing my elbow in the process. What a welcome!

I knew I'd done something really bad to my arm, so the next day I went to hospital for X-rays. 'It's fractured,' said the doctor. 'You need to put it in plaster, but we don't have any plaster.' He sent me to another hospital.

At the next hospital, the doctor said, 'You can't put that in plaster! That's not fractured, that's broken. It could easily swell up. I recommend you have the bone removed.' Remove the bone? That didn't sound right.

By this stage it was very late in the day. 'Let's go back to the house and regroup,' I said. So we drove home, along a road with a thousand curves and bumps, and I called a few friends for advice. 'Don't worry,' one mate said. 'I've got a great doctor friend in Maracay. He's got a private practice and does charity work, so he's really busy, but I'm sure he'll fit you in.'

I went to see the doctor in Maracay. 'That's definitely broken,' he said. 'We need to put a screw in it.' At last, a solution that sounded logical. 'But we can't operate for a couple of days,' he added.

So, four days after breaking my arm, I finally went into the operating theatre, having taken all my kit off and put on a little backless gown. It was particularly skimpy on me because it had been made for the average-sized South American patient.

I lay down on the operating table. The nurses turned up the salsa music on the big boogie box in the corner. Then the doctor appeared and produced a huge great screw for a joke. 'This is what we'll be using on your arm,' he laughed.

I woke up in total agony. Because it was a very poor charity hospital, there were no post-operative painkillers available, and someone had to run out and buy some.

The arm took a few weeks to heal, so for a while I was out of action in the

fields. Tania and I turned our attention to paperwork and tried to bring about a decision regarding the permissions for developing the farm into an eco-hotel. Frustratingly, they still hadn't come through, even though we'd produced proper building designs and plans, as requested. We went to Caracas and sat with a draughtsman for days on end designing all the different constructions.

Our research took us all around the city and to other cities: we even based our ideas for the main house on Simon Bolivar's beautiful colonial residence, Cagua. I think the delays to the permissions at this point occurred partly due to the looming spectre of a change of government. People wanted to see how the land would lie under a new president.

This meant that we couldn't move forward with our long-cherished project, which in turn had disastrous financial implications for us. We had investors lined up in Venezuela and the UK who believed in our project and were happy to fund it as soon as we got the go-ahead – but in the meantime, the farm was expensive to run and the cacao crop didn't yield enough to keep us going all year round. Replanting Zona 4 would increase our cacao output considerably, but only when the trees had matured. We needed other sources of income, and fast.

I looked into setting up a chocolate factory on the farm, but logistically it wasn't feasible: the climate wasn't right; the markets were elsewhere; it just wouldn't be profitable. So it seemed as if I was going to have to earn money another way before I went into chocolate-making. I was still determined to do it. It was just a question of how and when.

I tried to start up a range of moneymaking schemes: some worked, some failed. I bought lots of chickens and had plans to breed them and sell eggs; I

planted hundreds of cashew seeds (not realising how expensive a cashew-shelling machine would be); we sold nutmeg; we made mango and nutmeg jam; we sold the cacao bars; we ran the guesthouse; Tania ran a restaurant on the patio. We did anything we could, but it never seemed to be enough.

I realise now that when you move to a country like Venezuela, it's about quality of life, not making money – and we certainly had the most fantastic quality of life. When Tania's sister got married, we were stuck for a present. 'What can we give her?' Tania said. I suggested a set of drums, because we could source and make them ourselves.

In the dense jungle you can find hollow old trees, which are either dead, or dying, or hollowed out by ants. We found a fantastic toucajana trunk and made five drums out of it, three large and two small, with goat leather for the skins: a brilliant wedding present.

We raised our own pigs and fed them on the nuts that grew on the Mijau trees that shaded the cacao. The Spanish used the Mijau as shade trees because they produce a large nut that looks a bit like a broad bean and is ideal for pig food. I used to give the kids a bit of pocket money to collect Mijau seeds – it worked out cheaper than buying the artificial pig feed, which was horrible anyway, full of hormones and other nasty stuff. Incidentally, the Mijau fruit is about two inches long, pencil-shaped, reddish in colour and absolutely delicious. Collect enough of it and you can make a jam second to none.

We had a pig we called Mi Niña ('my child'); she was our great friend, almost completely domesticated. Mi Niña constantly battled with the Neapolitan mastiffs over food. Most of the time they got on fine, but there was mayhem whenever she raided one of their dog bowls. You'd hear the mastiffs desperately trying to get round the corner before she finished their food; in their haste they always ended up running on the spot, scraping their claws frantically on the shiny floor because they couldn't get a grip.

Sadly, Mi Niña became increasingly uncontrollable. She grew to several hundred kilos and charged around the house like some giant piglet. Then she had babies, and ate half of them, which we really couldn't bear; the second time she did it, we decided she had to go.

'Make it painless,' I said, handing Ricardo a sledgehammer.

'You mean, kill Mi Niña?' he said, raising his eyebrows in a way that couldn't help but make me feel guilty. Adding insult to injury, years later he told me he hadn't used the sledgehammer when he killed her. Instead, he'd done it like a professional and slit her throat with a knife.

Mi Niña was a pink American pig which should have had traditionally white, pork-style meat. However, because she'd been eating the Mijau nuts, her meat was a deep brown-red, more like wild boar. My sister, Sein, was staying with us when we ate Mi Niña and pronounced her the tastiest pig she'd ever tried, which was a huge accolade, because Sein is a successful chef with a very sophisticated palate.

At the end of 1998, Hugo Chavez won the presidential election and things began to change in Venezuela. The good news for us was that we finally got our permissions for everything, the following year. The Chavez government were very much in favour of the kind of development we were planning. Unfortunately, the economy started to slide and as a result there was a period of social instability. This affected us personally and in our business. Crime went up, tourism went down and we eventually had to advise our potential backers that it wasn't a secure time to invest in the project. The permissions had come too late.

We had a 4X4 stolen in Maracay; news of hold-ups and kidnap became more frequent. I said to Tania, 'I don't think you can go to Maracay on your own any more.' Being an independent woman, she was appalled. Until then, she had never thought twice about going around on her own.

Hang on a second, we thought. Can we really live here if we can't drive alone in the car? There were other factors, too. Our financial problems were

weighing us down. The children's education was also a concern. Sophia was getting to the age when she would soon be ready to go to school, and William was only two years behind her.

When Tania took the children back to England for a holiday, I began to think seriously about the future. I loved living on the farm more than anything, but I wanted what was best for my family. I sensed that Tania was feeling that our adventure hadn't worked and it was time to go home. It was hard to let the dream go, though. It was still so strong for me.

When Tania got back, we began to talk seriously about what we should do next. The thought of leaving El Tesoro was a terrible wrench, especially after all the fateful events that had led up to discovering the farm and buying it in the nick of time. We'd had the happiest times of our lives there. Our children had been born there; it was home. How could we bear to leave it behind? It was one of the most difficult things I've ever had to come to terms with.

Although we were in an economic depression in Venezuela, I felt adamant that you don't sell your dreams, and Tania agreed. Reluctantly we decided to go back to England, but to keep the farm on for as long as we could afford to. Tania and the kids went first, and I stayed on to tie up loose ends and find someone to manage the place.

I couldn't leave Bertillio in charge because by now he had started working for himself. 'Sometimes I want to wake up in the morning without having to go to work,' he'd explained, offering to help out whenever I needed him. He liked going to the mountains with his mules, taking cargo back and forth, so it made sense to scale down his farm workload to a couple of days a week.

I thought about employing a farm manager, but the people I interviewed just didn't seem to fit the bill. No one convinced me that they had the dedication needed to oversee the land and the cacao plantation.

One night, alone on the farm, I started to feel unwell. Then I developed a fever. When I started to have involuntary convulsions a couple of days later, I took myself to the hospital. 'Oh, you've got the local bug that's going around,' the doctor said casually. He gave me an injection and told me to stand under the shower for half an hour to bring my temperature down.

I felt a bit better after a shower; my temperature came down. But then it shot up again and the convulsions returned; I was overheating massively. My Swiss friend Emmanuel came up to the farm to see me. 'That's not a local fever,' he said. 'You've got something really bad. You need to get to a hospital.'

'I can't move, though,' I replied. By then I was about five days into it and I had such a bad headache that I couldn't move my head. It felt as if my brain was touching the inside of my skull.

Emmanuel rang my doctor in Caracas for advice. The doctor asked if I had any painkillers. Luckily, there were some leftover from the time I'd broken my arm. 'Give him one of those and take him straight to hospital,' my doctor said.

Emmanuel got me into the car and took me to Caracas, four hours away. It was impossible to park outside the hospital, so he pulled up at the door. I got out of the car and walked gingerly into the hospital foyer. The painkillers had worn off and I could barely move my head.

A nurse came rushing up to see what was wrong. 'Can we help you?'

All I could say was, 'My head, my head!'

The next day the doctors took samples from my spinal cord, extracting fluid from between my second and third vertebrae. Later I was diagnosed with viral meningitis and went on to spend several days in hospital. When I finally went home, I was thinner and a bit low on energy, but the doctors told me I'd make a full recovery. They were right – but they were wrong too. Unbeknownst to all, there were further repercussions on the way.

Back at the farm, the need to find a manager was becoming a matter of urgency. Who do I trust the most? I thought. And then it came to me: I trust Ricardo Soto, the man who has worked with me from the very beginning. 'Do you want the job?' I asked him. 'I'll pay you double. I'll give you a house. I'll pay all bills and electricity. You can have all the fruit off the farm while I'm not here, along with the proceeds of everything you sell, apart from the cacao. You can also keep your mules on the land and carry on doing your weekend work running mule trains from Cambalache.'

Ricardo handed the negotiations over to his wife, Annabel, and eventually the deal was done. Ricardo turned out to be the best choice I could have made for farm manager. He's looked after El Tesoro like it's his own property ever since.

I stayed on for an extra six months while Tania and the children were in England. I missed them like crazy, but there was a lot to sort out and I wanted to create more cacao planting programmes before I left. My plan was to run the farm with the income generated from the cacao harvests, so it was important to plant as many trees as possible.

One day I tweaked my back while Ricardo and I were chopping down a tree. Hmm, I thought, that feels pretty bad. My parents had come to stay and I was due to take them back to the airport later, so I went to the doctor for a painkiller.

Since he didn't have any pills in stock, the doctor gave me an injection in

the bum, which didn't make the four-hour drive to Caracas very comfortable. The road with its thousands of curves didn't do a lot for my back, either. The pain began to get worse. Soon it turned into the back pain from hell. By the time we got to the airport, it was so bad that I didn't know where to put myself.

'Mum, I've got to go,' I said, panicked by the pain.

I drove to Caracas, to my friend Tom Ashby's house, and called him from the car. 'Can you come and help me?' I said, gasping in agony. 'I can't get out of the car!'

It took forty-five minutes to get me into his house. It was madness; we kept laughing as he helped me move along, inch by inch. But laughing really hurt: I was half-laughing, half-crying.

Finally I made it inside and lay on the floor for a rest. 'Shit, Willie, I'm going on holiday tomorrow,' Tom said. 'This is terrible timing. What are you going to do?'

'I'll be okay,' I said. 'It should be better by the morning.' I went to get up and pour myself a glass of water, but suddenly I couldn't move. At all.

And that was that: I didn't move from the floor for the next ten days. It was horrible and I got very, very depressed, lying on the floor in phenomenal agony, seeing no one except a guy who came up from the farm to bring me food. It was definitely one of the low points of my life.

When I finally managed to get to hospital, an MRI scan showed that I had two slipped discs and a hernia on one of them – in the exact same place that I'd had fluid extracted during the tests to diagnose my viral meningitis, which obviously wasn't a coincidence.

When I was up and moving again, I went back to the farm to oversee one final harvest before leaving for England. But then disaster struck. A dry winter turned into a desperate winter drought and we started to lose trees. It was incredibly distressing. Waiting for rain day in day out was just soul-destroying.

In farming, you tend to learn by your mistakes and make up for them in the following years. However, some things are totally out of your control: there's nothing you can do to change the course of nature. So even though we were irrigating the plantation with waterways, we went on to lose around 3,000 trees. I was devastated, because I'd put so much work into them.

I suppose at that point the easiest option would have been to go home and forget all about it – I was due to leave very soon anyway. But that just wasn't my style. So I made the long journey back to Felix in Costa Maya, bought another load of seeds and painstakingly replanted them before I went back to England. I was determined not to give up on my dreams, no matter what life threw at me.

Left: Ricardo and me

Chapter 5

I Build
a Chocolate Factory

Back in England, I discovered the internet. Since I'd never even turned on a computer before 2001, this was a huge technological leap. It was amazing to find a whole world of specialist second-hand machine dealers out there in cyberspace, and people from Germany to America selling roasters and grinders! I surfed, I searched, I emailed. I drove the dealers crazy with my questions and low budget.

I really missed Venezuela, but being in England began to make sense. My mission suddenly became clear to me: I'd build the chocolate factory in Devon instead of Choroni. I'd woo the UK with my cacao. I was going to revolutionise the nation's palate and bring back real chocolate, with all its true flavour and benefits.

For now, though, this would remain my secret passion. In the meantime, Tania and I had to support our family and keep the hacienda going. We ran a family project in Devon and I did all kinds of different work, from painting and decorating to gardening and event organising. Sometimes I cooked for more than a hundred people, for weddings and other occasions.

It was tough going and no matter how hard I seemed to work, we were always stretched for cash. Every spare bit of money went towards paying my workers at El Tesoro. I was keeping my dream alive, but only just.

I knew that to start my project, I had to have a roaster, a winnower, a grinder and a conching machine. Eventually I flew to Bilbao and visited a chocolate factory in Zaragoza in Northern Spain. The company that owned the factory had never thrown away or sold any of their machinery; now they were moving to a modern building and space was an issue, so they were selling a load of machines off cheaply. It seemed like a great opportunity.

I was disappointed when I got there, though, because the machinery was just too old. It was like walking around a museum. There was a hoard of machines that dated from the late 1800s and some that dated back to the 1850s. Unfortunately, most of them were so rusty or broken up that they were beyond my mending capabilities.

Then, just as I was leaving, I noticed an old 1940–50s cacao winnower in the corner. It had fallen over, probably off the forklift, and was slightly bent, but I could tell that it wasn't beyond repair. I can fix that, I thought. I wasn't sure what was exactly wrong with it, but the problem was purely mechanical, so it wouldn't be too difficult to sort out. Rather than leave empty-handed, I offered the dealer 1,000 euros for it. I got it for 1,500 euros: a quarter of the price it would have fetched in working order.

Feeling a lot happier, I arranged for the winnower to be shipped back to my mum's house in Wales. Mum agreed to store it in a shed, where it would sit until I found the other pieces. I assured Mum that one day I'd take it away again, and to her credit she believed me. I've always been a dreamer and my chocolate factory project must have seemed like another of my dreams.

Whenever I could, I flew back to Venezuela to oversee the cacao harvests and make cacao bars to sell downtown. I always brought a bundle of bars back to England with me. I couldn't do without them in my cooking and now my friends and family were clamouring for them too. Everyone was getting into cacao's energy-boosting properties; I kept hearing what a great pick-me-up it was during the afternoon slump.

While I was still away, Tania had given a couple of my cacao bars to her old school friend, Alice Brown. It just so happened that Alan Porter, who owned the Chocolate Society, noticed them when he visited her house. The Chocolate Society was a chocolate company with a reputation for selling the finest chocolate – they even sold online – and Alan was highly respected in the chocolate world. He had introduced high quality French chocolate to the UK: he sold it to chefs and used it to make his own delicious chocolate delights.

'Where did those cacao bars come from?' he asked Alice.

'Willie makes them,' she said. 'He'll be back from South America soon.'

When I got back from Venezuela, Alan wanted to meet me, so Alice came for dinner one night bringing Alan and his wife Sally. Alan and I immediately got on and he soon became my chocolate guru. Naturally, he was intrigued to hear about the farm, the plantation, my replanting programmes and cacao-making activities, and he was very keen to try my truffles.

The next time I went to Venezuela, he told me to bring him some cacao bars to trial and sell through the Chocolate Society. I made three kinds: plain; with cloud forest papelon sugar; and with chilli. My dream of making my own chocolate in England was coming closer to being reality. It was very encouraging that someone like Alan rated my cacao enough to sell it.

While I was at the farm, he put me in contact with a chocolatier called Linny Gentle-Cadeau. Linny was about to leave her job in Geneva and was thinking of starting work at the Chocolate Society, but first she wanted to take some time off, travel a bit and visit a cacao plantation. 'Come and stay!' I told her. 'You'll be here in time for the harvest.'

Linny loved the farm and Choroni, and when it was time for the cacao

harvest, she came along with the boys to give a hand with pulling the pods off the trees. The process of harvesting, fermenting and drying seemed to fascinate her. She is passionate about food, so we spent a lot of time cooking. We made chicken mole, fish soups, fish marinades, vanilla and chocolate ice cream and lots of chocolate cakes.

Once the beans were dried, I set about making hundreds of cacao bars in the kitchen, as usual, and Linny helped out. We spent hours and hours experimenting with roasting times and different beans – 20 minutes… 21 minutes… 25 minutes – tasting the flavour variations and trying to decide which was better.

Having Linny at the farm was brilliant, and it seemed like the ideal moment to try and make a bar of actual chocolate – after all, here was a bona fide chocolatier to help.

First we needed cacao butter. At this point, I didn't have the press I needed to extract the butter from my own liquor, so I was pretty pleased when I managed to source some cacao butter locally. I took it back to the farm. 'What's that?' Linny asked.

I looked down at the tub of bright, white, lardy fat. 'Isn't it deodorised cacao butter?' I said.

'Definitely not. It's too white,' she said. It turned out to be sheep or goat's fat, a huge disappointment.

Next we went to a shop in downtown Maracay that one of my workers had recommended. A bit seedy and mysterious, with iron bars on the windows, it was a funny old place that didn't seem to sell anything in particular, but was full of herbs, bric-a-brac, voodoo and religious paraphernalia and medicine bottles. It certainly wasn't the kind of shop where you expected to find cacao butter. But this time we found what we were looking for and went home happy.

Back at the farm, we played around with different quantities of cacao liquor, cacao butter and sugar. We didn't know the exact proportions to put in, so Linny texted her friends in Switzerland who made chocolate: 'How much cacao mass, sugar and cacao butter?' There wasn't a mobile phone signal at the farm, so every time we had a question, we went down the mountain to Choroni to send a text, and they went back down again later to pick up the reply.

We tried several ways of incorporating the sugar into the mixture without losing the smooth texture. There was no possibility of conching anything, because we didn't have the equipment, so we ended up with something that was fairly coarse. However, we did eventually manage to get something that had a bit of a snap to it.

We moulded lots of bars in little Tupperware boxes and made impressions of leaves and cacao pods on top of them. It was thrilling: my first ever bars of chocolate! They retained most of the flavour notes of the 100 per cent unrefined cacao, but were sweeter and a lot less coarse. After we tried them for the first time, we danced around the kitchen and I sang a spontaneous chocolate bar song. It really felt like another important step on my chocolate journey.

For years I had been following what was happening in the chocolate world, from the rise of percentage chocolate to the new 'good' American chocolate and the edgy young companies producing it. There's a new chocolate movement sweeping America. Here, it's more than a niche club and there's change on the horizon.

I'd always had it in mind to meet Rose Gray after making her Nemesis with my cacao, so when I got back to England I went to see her at the River Café in London. We had a chat, she was very charming and I gave her a bar of cacao, curious about what someone of her calibre would think of it. 'I believe it would make a fantastic Nemesis!' I told her.

Six months later, my sister Sein bought me a book written by Chantelle Cody. 'Willie, it's really curious…' she said, showing me a passage where Chantelle Cody talks about how she had a meeting with Rose Gray. At the meeting, Rose had apparently produced some very raw, very obviously high quality cacao that had very interesting aromas: my cacao! I've since sent her a case of my very latest Carenero.

In early 2006, I met up with my friend Jim Bellieni, a photographer who has also worked in TV and as a promo director. Over a beer I reminisced about my life on the farm, the cooking I'd done and my adventures with cacao. When I mentioned that the next harvest was due in February, his eyes lit up. 'We should make a film about it!' he said.

Jim was a huge inspiration. He came out to Choroni for the harvest and directed and shot reams of great footage. He filmed from dawn till dusk, covered every stage of the process and gave me loads of advice and tips about how to appear on camera. The idea was to produce a pilot programme with my American friend Tom Vogel (the guy who had nearly drowned at Lejau). 'Bean to Bar: Jungle Cooking' was supposed to be a cooking comedy set on the hacienda, a two-hander featuring an English guy and an American, the US element giving us the added possibility of selling it in America.

One day while we were filming in the kitchen, I spotted a small green snake behind the washing machine. I grabbed it by its tail, pulled it out from its hiding place and gently swung it in the air.

'This is one of the most dangerous snakes in Venezuela!' I said. At which Jim promptly dropped the camera.

It was an escapade gone badly wrong – the camera lay on the floor with the microphone bent to one side – and after that, the sound didn't work very well. This unfortunately ruined a lot of the scenes featuring Tom, who arrived from New York after the damage had been done.

Three weeks later, Jim and I returned to England with six large coolers of cacao bars that we'd made during the filming. It seemed the perfect moment to trial my cacao; I had to know that there would be a demand for it before I could think seriously about producing it commercially. After all, it's one thing to dream and quite another for people to buy into your dream.

First I delivered a batch to my great friend Marco Pierre White, who had constantly encouraged me in my chocolate adventure and was a big fan of my cacao. Marco and I met in London back in our teens, when he was a trainee chef in Oxford. Someone introduced us at Pucci's pizzeria on the King's Road and we had a long chat one night in a club called Crazy Larry's. We bonded and have stayed so ever since.

Marco was always there on the end of the phone, being positive. He has supported me every step of the way. Another great support was our friend Caroline True. I asked Caroline if she would try selling my cacao in her chichi delicatessen in Somerset and she agreed to give it a go. She immediately began stocking it and the response from her customers was amazing.

The Chocolate Society were already selling it through their shops and online. Next I went to a chocolate emporium in Notting Hill called Melt, which is owned by Louise Nason. Louise is the genuine article: she is absolutely passionate about chocolate, puts flavour before shelf life and produces wonderful, romantic chocolates. Soon after I visited Louise, I was introduced to Petra Barran, who runs a chocolate business from her mobile chocolate van and is on her own unique chocolate vibe.

I felt I had covered all bases: the top chef; the smart chocolate shop; the Chocolate Society; the chichi country deli and Petra, the wacky Choc Star. They all bought my cacao and everyone loved it. Petra's clients were even blogging about my hot chocolate online. This is great! I thought. Let's go! My market research had been a success and I felt I had the assurances I needed to push forward and get my cacao business up and running. Very kindly, my family helped me to make a start. I'm very aware of how incredibly lucky I've been to have such a great family behind me.

The next step was to source and buy the machines. The roaster was key – after fermentation, roasting is the next most important stage in developing the unique flavour and aroma of the beans. High quality beans don't need heavy roasting, but a light roast takes the flavour to another level.

I already had the sheller, sitting in a shed at my mum's. The sheller winnows the beans to produce cacao nibs, the edible part of the bean. Then the nibs go through a grinder, which releases the cacao butter, now liquefied, and then it drops on to the rollers of a refiner. The rollers catch the smooth cacao liquid, draw it up and refine it so that it runs smoothly off into containers. The refined liquid cacao mass is then ready for conching, which is another key stage in developing the flavour. The conching machine agitates the cacao mass, which removes the bitterness and brings out the intense flavour notes.

In Aztec drawings, you often see people pouring *xocolatl* from a great height into a bowl below, where it forms a frothy mass. This appears to be a very natural way of conching, of aerating and agitating the warm cacao to remove its bitterness. The conching machine I was looking for would mechanise that process.

For years I had been quietly researching all the machine outlets. When I heard about a company in Germany with a 1920s roaster and a concher that sounded promising, I booked a flight and went to take a look. I naturally kept cool about what I was interested in: I had entered the world of buying second-hand machinery! I paid casual attention to the roaster as I wandered around the warehouse. It was an ancient piece of kit and had what looked like an old bicycle chain on the back of it. Apparently, it had been used for roasting almonds, which made sense when I looked inside it, because it was very clean and smooth, whereas the acidity of cacao causes pitting. I knew I could fix it. Yes, I thought, I'll have that, but they were asking too much for it.

The conching machines were damaged and covered in chocolate. I could see that one side was broken up and the bearings had gone, but it wasn't a disaster. The problems were all mechanical, so I knew I could mend it.

Aware that very few people would want to buy this kind of antique machinery, I went back to England without sealing the deal and we batted our negotiations back and forth by email and phone. They cleaned the conching tanks for another prospective buyer and copied me in on the photos. I could now see there were cracks in the rollers.

'Those cracks have been there for years – the tanks will work for another hundred years,' they assured me. 'Anyway, someone else is interested in them.'

'Oh really?' I said, feigning a lack of interest.

I stuck to my guns and eventually they accepted my offer. It was a great result for me, and probably a good deal for them as well. Those machines could have stayed in the warehouse for years if I hadn't bought them, mainly because they would never have passed Health and Safety in the state they were in.

I rang round several estate agents looking for a unit where I could set up the factory, but soon realised that I didn't have that kind of money. Then someone gave me a number and said, 'Ring these guys: they've got some old chicken sheds and a lot of people get started there.' So I rang them. They not only had chicken sheds, but something for everyone's pocket, new and old.

All that was missing now was a grinder and a tempering machine. I also needed a bigger injection of cash, so I set about writing a business plan, with the help of my accountant.

The bank genuinely seemed to understand my business concept, and appreciated that it was the right time to launch a 100 per cent cacao bar. I already had the premises and the machines (the bank didn't know what state they were in!); I had put in some of my own money; I'd done my market research

and had a letter from Marco Pierre White confirming future orders. Now I needed a loan to get the business off the ground. As it turned out, the amount I asked for was a bit of an underestimation, although not a gross underestimation, thankfully. The point was, the bank backed my dream and I got the loan. I was on my way.

But there was still so much to do, from building the factory to reconditioning the machines. Still, I could only take things step-by-step. In the back of my head I sensed that the delivery of the beans was going to be my main problem, but I had to believe that everything would all work out okay. In order to keep going, I had to keep believing.

Since the crop on my farm wasn't big enough to provide the number of beans I needed for the volume of cacao bars I was planning to produce, I needed to source other high quality beans. So, when I went to Venezuela in the autumn of 2006 to arrange for the export of my El Tesoro beans, I planned to explore the possibilities of finding other beans as well.

It should have been a fairly simple process. As a cacao farmer, I was permitted to buy and export cacao; it was just a case of doing the paperwork. But suddenly it all became very difficult. Initially, the people working in the cacao markets agreed to sell me the beans I wanted, but when I turned up to negotiate, they changed their minds. Others said they would export my El Tesoro beans, but when I went to see them, they said they wouldn't. Uncertain of where to turn next, I had to face the terrifying prospect of having a chocolate factory, but no beans. It was unthinkable!

For the moment, I was stuck. There was nothing for it but to take my destiny into my own hands, so I went on a cross-country trip to source my own beans, taking a cast-iron pan, a fan and a small grinder with me. My plan was to hand-process and taste cacao beans at every hacienda I visited; the most effective way to gauge the unique flavour, subtle taste notes and quality of the beans was to make a truffle mix using sugar and a local type of cream.

I decided to focus on two distinct Trinitario strains: Carenero and Rio Caribe. My friend John Kehoe had recommended Carenero, which has a nutty, spicy flavour. I'd also come across it in my travels around Venezuela and read about it. Rio Caribe was another delicious strain, famous for its citrus notes, and I felt it made a good contrast with the Carenero.

My neighbour's farm manager came from Barlovento, a stretch of coast about two hours east of Caracas that is well known for growing Carenero. I rang him and said, 'I'm coming to Barlovento. Can I meet you? Perhaps you can help me with sourcing beans?'

'Of course!' he said. I set off with Teting, an old friend who lives on a small farm in Choroni. Teting had friends of friends who owned cacao plantations and might also be able to help us.

On our way to Barlovento, we stopped off for a break in a tiny little town. As we stretched our legs in the main square, we noticed a beautiful eighteenth-century church. Inside the church, there were workers restoring the roof.

'Hi, what brings you guys here?' one of the roofers called out.

'We're buying cacao beans,' I explained.

'Have you spoken to Pedro, then?' he said.

'Who's Pedro?' I asked.

'Who's Pedro?' he repeated, laughing. 'Pedro has a chocolate factory!'

Intrigued, we followed the tangent. The roofer took us to meet Pedro, who turned out to be a passionate chocolate-maker who had built his own mini-chocolate factory in his house. It was all quite remarkable. Pedro's cacao-processing machines were made on a perfect, miniature scale. There was a mini cocoa press, a mini roaster and a tiny sheller. The roaster was a converted coffee roaster. The press was an adapted car jack that squashed a tube that squeezed out cocoa butter. The winnower was a sweet but efficient little nut sheller. The chocolate was moulded in a small, cool room in the centre of the house. All in the middle of nowhere!

Pedro was a beautifully romantic figure, in his sixties and incredibly sincere. We spent three hours talking chocolate with him, sitting on vinyl sofas in his front room. There was a little display cabinet against one wall, showing off half a dozen of the delicious 'bon-bons' he made – exquisite little chocolate balls with fresh papaya in the centre.

Pedro sold his chocolate locally, but had recently hooked up with some Belgian guys who had stumbled across him by chance, as we had. He had just started making 100 per cent cacao and exporting it. We swapped stories about

Right: Pedro Martinez, Venezuelan Chocolatier

the bureaucracy involved in the export business and joked about how crazy and difficult the paperwork was. I understood exactly where he was coming from: he was trying to export the liquor to Europe; I was trying to buy beans to make liquor in Europe. We were both part of the same cacao dream.

Meeting Pedro was inspirational. As we talked, I remembered that I had lots of beautiful chocolate moulds at home that I'd picked up on one of my mad trips to an old Terry's chocolate factory. There were lovely trays of love hearts and diamonds, and they were proper long-lasting hard moulds, not the flimsy kind you get today. So when we left, I said, 'Pedro, I'm coming back and I'm going to bring some chocolate moulds that will be perfect for you.' He gave me one of his broad, open smiles and wished us well on our journey.

Teting and I drove on. We stopped off in a tiny place where I'd arranged to speak to a local farmer about the price of Carenero and the state of the latest crop. Then we headed towards Rio Caribe, a further eight hours from Barlovento.

Just outside Rio Caribe, we rocked up at the Hacienda Bucari, a cacao farm that also ran a guesthouse, or posada, for tourists. Its owner had built a chocolate factory and attached it to the farm; he was one step up from Pedro because he had a small 500-kilo conch refiner and a tempering machine. It was still an artisan's approach to making chocolate – it wasn't anywhere near to being an automated plant – but he had the proper machines with which to make his milk and dark chocolate bars and bon-bons.

He showed us around the factory and kindly offered to put us in touch with some very small cacao co-operatives. Next, Teting and I visited a local co-operative in Rio Caribe, where the farmers agreed to supply me with beans. We took some samples and left feeling optimistic, but I wasn't happy with the next lot of samples they sent, so I didn't take it any further.

I had decided from the start of this trip to Venezuela that I was going to follow every possible path and possibility. I didn't want to go back to England and think, I wish I'd pursued this lead, or that strand! So I went down every avenue I found until I came to the end and knew what was there. And if there was nothing there, I went down the next one.

One particular avenue took us to just outside Puerto Cabello, where we met up with some cacao farmers on their farm. 'Are you ready to see the most beautiful cacao plantation in the world?' said our host, a weathered farmer with a twinkle in his eye.

'There you'll find cacao like no other!' said one of his workers, rather poetically I thought.

'And after you've seen his plantation, I'll take you to my plantation,' said another farmer. 'My cacao is even better than his!' he declared proudly, puffing up his chest.

A group of us mounted some mules and rode high up into the mountains. The further we climbed, the more my anticipation grew. In my mind's eye, I envisaged a secret 'El Dorado' of cacao, a natural treasure trove – a treasure grove, with gigantic, juicy pods hanging from beautiful, healthy trees that grew beneath a vast network of mighty shade canopies.

Nothing could have been further from the truth. The moment we reached the first farmer's plantation I could see that the cacao was barely growing in the shade; the trees were just about alive; and the beans were small, rotten and fungus-ridden. What a disaster. I felt badly let down.

'This is a non-runner,' I told Teting. 'That's how NOT to grow cacao. Let's go.'

'No!' the second farmer said. 'You must come on to see my plantation! It's only another half an hour further and it's so much better than this one.'

We tried to be polite, but I knew a dead end when I saw one. Another half an hour to get there meant another half an hour back, which would put an extra hour on the journey. We were already many hours away from Caracas and I wasn't prepared to waste any more time. 'Sorry, guys, we've got to head back

now,' I said firmly. We left them arguing on the patio.

It was all part of the trip: to know and understand cacao better. That day I learned that not everyone who grows it knows how to grow it.

Back in Caracas and now desperate for beans, I was introduced to an important cacao broker. 'I really need a hand,' I explained to him. 'First of all, I only want to buy six tons of beans.'

He raised his eyebrows. I knew that he wouldn't be interested in such a small order. It was nothing to him, less than peanuts. 'But my next order will be for twelve and a half tons,' I rapidly assured him, 'and after that I'll need regular shipments of twenty-five tons. I've got the factory and the machinery, but I can only afford to start off with a small order.'

I sensed that the big bean brokers appreciated that the big chocolate companies had dictated cacao prices for too long, so I said, 'The more buyers you've got, the more potential you have to push the prices up, and the more you can play one buyer off against another. It's just good business.'

He frowned. I could tell that he was listening intently. 'Anyway, what have you got to lose?' I went on. 'Okay, processing one container is as much work as processing three. But if you can bring yourself another buyer who will help you push prices up, you win in the end.'

He gave it some thought and came back to me. 'Yes, I will do it,' he said. 'Bring your beans to me and I will do the rest.'

It was a huge relief. Not only was he going to ship my El Tesoro beans to England, he would also source high quality Carenero and Rio Caribe beans for export. After three months of uncertainty in Venezuela, I could return to England and get on with building the factory.

Unfortunately, the bean saga wasn't quite over. I managed to get back to Tania and the children in the nick of time for Christmas in England, only to find out the following April – four whole months of waiting later – that the arrangement with the big Caracas broker wasn't going to happen. My shipment wasn't on its way after all! I could hardly believe it when I finally realised that he had strung me along and wasn't going to deliver.

Whether this was because he was also working for a well-known European chocolate company, I can never be certain. All I know is that I was going crazy waiting for those beans! After all, what good was a chocolate factory if I couldn't make chocolate? I was at my wits' end.

To make matters worse – but better too, in a way – I'd had a big break regarding the film Jim had shot at the farm the previous year. In the twelve months since it had been made, no one had managed to find anyone to edit it. Finally I rang a director friend and asked for his help. 'I've got to get this edited!' I told him. 'We can't leave the project unfinished.'

A few weeks later, he called back. 'I've managed to pull a favour for you,' he said. 'There's an assistant in an edit suite called Final Cut who says he'll edit the film for you.'

So I went along and met Eddie Cheeseman, who had decided to help us out purely because he liked the film and believed in our idea. I supplied him with some tapes of music – that a couple of musician friends had sourced – and within a few weeks he had produced six minutes of fantastic footage with a great soundtrack. (The only downside was that a lot of the footage featuring Tom and me together had been ruined by sound problems, so it didn't work as a two-hander.) I touted it around to a couple of production companies and suddenly everybody wanted it. It was a really exciting breakthrough: it looked like I was in with a chance of having a television programme made about my cacao.

However, things weren't looking so good in other departments. In fact, the whole chocolate-making project was teetering on the brink, which was more than slightly worrying. Although my dream was still as strong as ever, the reality was showing cracks: the factory was far from finished; my machines were mostly in bits; and I still didn't have any beans!!!! I definitely didn't want a TV company documenting any of that.

What on earth was I going to do?

Right: Bean testing at Hacienda San José

Chapter 6

Viva Cacao!
The Food of the Gods

The pressure was on. Some weeks I was working twelve hours a day, every day. There was so much to do: I had to design and build the factory from scratch (along with a local builder, Bob Browning); I had to recondition the machines I had already bought, and source new machines in the UK and Europe; there were labels to be designed; I had to think about packaging and supply routes; and it was time to start spreading the word of what I was doing to potential buyers. It was a constant juggling process. Every day there seemed to be a new challenge.

I hardly spent any time at home and I really missed Tania and the children. So when I did manage to snatch the odd day off, we tried to make the most of it. On William's birthday I bought him a fishing rod and we went fly-fishing at a little trout fishery near our house. Together we caught a three and a half pound trout, which made our day!

There are certain occasions that just can't be missed, no matter how busy you are. Especially birthdays and Christmas. Sophia wanted a sleepover with her friends on her birthday, so I took a few hours off to help Tania make a mountain of rich chocolate brownies and fairy cakes for them all. Meanwhile, little Evie, our youngest child, is mad about making and eating truffles, so that's always her special treat; she's never happier than when she's in the kitchen helping Tania or me make another batch.

Tania's truffles are the best. Every time I go to Venezuela to oversee the cacao harvest at the farm, I bring back a bottle of the best rum. Tania soaks her truffle raisins in it, sometimes for as long as a couple of weeks. Then she mashes them through the truffle mix to make a heady concoction of chocolate, fruit and alcohol. From Choroni to Devon, everyone loves her rum and raisin truffles.

Tania also makes a mean Cloud Forest Chocolate Cake. It was one of the first cacao recipes I developed and it's a real attention-grabber. In Venezuela, around the middle of December, I'd give it a seasonal twist and turn it into Willie's Chocolate Christmas Cake: the trick was to soak some sultanas in cognac, drain them and stire them into the cake mix before baking. Then I added the leftover cognac to the truffle mix icing. Zing!

Late December in the tropics is great. It's a month into the dry season but the countryside is still beautiful, lush and green, and there's a refreshing breeze in the air. It's a very family-oriented time in South America and Choroni is totally empty – apart from the locals – which makes it a very special time of year.

The classic Venezuelan festive season dish is the hallaca, which is typically a mixture of chicken, beef, pork, onions, tomatoes, capers, raisins and olives parcelled with a maize dough and wrapped and bound in a banana leaf. This is

the one time of the year that everybody harvests the banana leaf, particularly the purple leaves from the morada bananas. You see people standing by the side of the road selling them; it's a tradition all over Venezuela.

Every year Tania used to make a whole load of hallacas and freeze them, so that whenever anyone came to see us over the Christmas period, we could take some out of the freezer, boil them up in a big pan of water and offer them round. If you're stingy with the mixture, they're not very good. But if you keep the dough thin and add cacao for extra richness, as we did, they are absolutely delicious.

My passion for chocolate knows no bounds! I grate cacao into curries, stews, roasted vegetables, risottos and all kinds of desserts. Every morning I fry my eggs in chilli oil and sprinkle a layer of grated cacao on top. It's a delicious combination, but it only works with chilli oil, which you can easily make yourself by soaking some dried chillies in olive oil or sunflower oil. I can't have my fried eggs any other way at the moment – they're absolutely addictive.

I love the thought that I'm just one chocolate lover in a long history of passionate chocoholics. One of my favourite stories is the one about the 17th century Bishop of Chiapas in Mexico, who decided that chocolate broke the rules of fasting and threatened his parishioners with excommunication if they drank it during the celebration of mass. He was promptly found dead, allegedly killed by the chocolate-mad women of his congregation, who sent him a gift of poisoned cacao. A Mexican proverb referring to this incident still survives today: 'Beware the chocolate of Chiapas'.

Eventually Pope Alexander VII stepped in and gave chocolate the holy thumbs up by saying, 'Liquidum non frangit jejunum' ('Liquids do not break the fast'). Something tells me he would have had a mass uprising on his hands if he hadn't let it go.

Although Tania loves cacao as much as I do and has wholeheartedly embraced it in her cooking, she's not so happy that it has managed to permeate our entire house, from floor to ceiling. I'm always covered in cacao when I get home from the factory. It's in my hair, on my face and arms, under my fingernails and all over my clothes. As a result, it's on everything, from our sheets and towels to the carpet. When I take my clothes off, they're stiff with cacao; they practically stand up in the wash basket. Every couple of weeks one of us has to scrape a thick layer of cacao butter from the inside of the washing machine.

I've stopped noticing that there's cacao everywhere, and I never tire of experimenting. Recently I got home after work to find Tania had made a fantastic chicken and vegetable soup. After we'd each had a bowl, I said, 'Let's try it with cacao!' I grated some into the leftovers and we sat down again to taste it. Her soup was already sublime, so it didn't make it better, but it did make it different, somehow richer.

Whenever I get a bit tired at the factory, or something goes wrong, I make a traditional Venezuelan hot chocolate, which is a combination of water, cacao and sugar heated up in a pan. Sometimes I make it with honey, because it brings out a slightly different flavour note. When I haven't got time to boil the kettle, I break a chunk off a bar of cacao and chew on it – I don't care if it's not sweet, it gives me GO! I've come to rely on that 100 per cent cacao boost over the past eighteen months.

There were so many times when I thought I wouldn't make it, when it looked like the whole project was going to crumble before my eyes. As the months dragged on and still no beans arrived, I began to go crazy with worry. I literally didn't have a bean in the world, as the expression goes. It was a hair-pulling time.

Words cannot express how I felt when John Kehoe called to say that he had found me another bean broker – and not just any broker, but the three Francesci brothers, the only grower-brokers in Venezuela. John had persuaded them to ship my El Tesoro harvest and supply me with three tons of Rio Caribe and three tons of Carenero.

Absolutely passionate about chocolate, the Francescis are always researching new ways to ferment cacao and new techniques to improve production and flavour. There's something very romantic about three brothers all being so intensely involved in chocolate; in fact the entire family is mad about cacao. They've even got nieces and cousins doing university doctorates in it. So I knew immediately I was in the right hands. These people weren't solely focused on money. They had a genuine interest in improving cacao and chocolate production; they grew their own Rio Caribe along with a range of varieties sourced from all over Venezuela.

After more than six months of rising anxiety levels over the lack of beans, my supply problems had finally been resolved. I was incredibly grateful to John, who has since left broking to take over bean sourcing and farmer relations at a cutting-edge chocolate company in America. I don't know what I would have done without him. At last I was getting my heart's desire: three distinct bean types, each from a different region of Venezuela, with flavour notes that reflected their individual habitats, from tree and soil to climate.

But for every up, there was a down. The day the roaster arrived at the factory was a real low point: it turned up in bits and as I started to assemble it, I

Above: Drying patios at Hacienda San José

realised the heat exchanger was missing. It was a horrible moment. How was I going to roast my beans without an oven? The clock was ticking and I was running out of options. I suppose I could have sent the roaster back to Germany, but then I wouldn't have had one at all. I urgently had to get it working. It was time to improvise, and be quick about it.

With the help of my good friend and neighbour, Brian King, I drew a plan of a substitute oven that we could make using the end of a large pipe, with a stainless-steel inner sleeve that would withstand high temperatures. I gave Brian the bits and he skilfully assembled them. Our makeshift oven roaster worked really well at first, but then the heat exchanger started overheating.

Meanwhile, I was ringing the dealers in Germany almost every day.

'Have you found the oven unit yet?'

'Are you sure it didn't arrive?' they kept asking.

'*!$%!!?*!yes!' I insisted.

I didn't give up. I called again and again, and my persistence paid off, because eventually they found it. It had been in the warehouse all along, but marked as part of the wrong lot number. I was really relieved when it arrived. At last I had a roaster that worked properly. Next I picked up the winnower from my mum's shed in Wales.

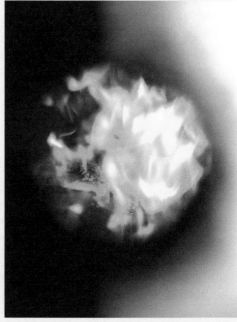

Once the beans have been lightly roasted, they drop into a vat. A cyclone draws air out, cooling them down; from there they go into the winnower, which smashes them and drops the cacao nibs on to a table that vibrates and grades them by size. The shells are sucked away by another cyclone and ejected out of the window into a big dumper bag.

At the end of the day, I sling the shells in the back of my Volvo, take them home and put them on my vegetable garden. I also give them to a local market gardener in exchange for vegetables. 3 per cent of cacao is vitamins and minerals and there are traces of that goodness in the shells, which are considered to be a three-in-one fertiliser. In Venezuela, they help to enrich the forest floor; in Devon, they provide nutritious food for our gardens. I love the fact that they don't go to waste.

When the shells have been discarded, the cacao nibs go into the mill, where two big granite stones grind together to crush them. This produces heat that helps to evaporate the bitterness and melt the cacao butter. About 50 per cent of cacao is made up of cacao butter.

The cacao and the cacao butter drop out of the grinder in a coarse liquid form down on to a refiner, which is comprised of three rollers. What's great about my old 1940s refiner machine is that it's so old-fashioned it's manually

adjustable, which means I can squeeze the rollers together to get a really fine finish. The chocolate runs off it like a river.

At first, I thought I might be able to do without a refiner, because in Venezuela I had been able to mill the cacao so that it was fine enough to do without. However, after I took a sample to William Curley, the renowned chocolatier, I changed my mind. Although he heaped praise on the flavours and richness of my cacao, he expressed doubts about whether it was refined enough for the mainstream market. I have a lot of respect for William's talent and expertise, so I took his advice on board.

Next: the conching refiner – something Linny and I were lacking in Venezuela when we made my first chocolate. It's an absolutely crucial piece of kit in the factory.

After the soft-state cacao runs off the refiner rollers into a tub, it is then tipped into the warm water-lagged longitudinal conching tanks of my conch refiner. Granite rollers weighing 150 kilos roll back and forth for eight to twelve hours on a granite base to further refine the cacao mass, agitating it to help remove bitterness and bring out the uniquely intense flavours of the cacao. A central motor spins the flywheels, which draw the rollers back and forth.

Although they're absolutely ancient, my longitudinal conching tanks are the Rolls Royce of chocolate-making machines. I bought them broken and worn, and commissioned a local engineering firm to make some replacement parts. It's a big hi-tech firm of engineers and this wasn't a great money-spinner for them, but they were happy to help out. I think they enjoyed doing the work and they liked the story too. Everywhere I went, I tried to spread my passion for chocolate. 'This is the mission…!' I would start. I was selling them my chocolate dream. And people seemed to go with it.

The first time the conch refiner turned over, it made a hell of a racket; it was banging and clanging like crazy. I turned it off, wondering what on earth could be wrong: it turned out that all the rollers were on the wrong arms and in the wrong tanks. Once I'd fixed that particular problem, I realised that there were lots of holes in the water tanks, so Brian came down with his welding kit and welded them shut. Thinking we'd sealed all of them, we filled the tanks up with water. But we'd missed some – they were plugged with chocolate – so when we turned on the machine, the water exploded out of them and the effect was of a mechanical, many-spouted whale!

The whole thing had to be dismantled and put back together again. It was incredibly dispiriting and time-consuming. I drank literally gallons of hot

Left: Grinding and refining

chocolate over that time, just to keep me going.

As with the roasting, I make sure not to over-conch the cacao. Some chocolatiers might conch for days, which results in very smooth and glutinous cacao, but loses a lot of the flavours – whereas I try to keep as many of those interesting flavours in, while taking the unpalatable edge off. I lightly conch to aerate the chocolate, warm it and get rid of the bitterness, while retaining the zing and goodness. Fine beans especially don't need a lot of conching. Criollo and Trinitario beans are nothing like as bitter as the more mass-produced Forestera type.

If you look at old photos of Fry's and Cadbury's factories, you'll see that once upon a time there were warehouses with hundreds of conching machines like mine, rows upon rows of them. The noise must have been deafening and the smell of chocolate totally overpowering.

Once the beans have been harvested, fermented, dried, shipped, roasted, shelled, ground, refined and conched, there is one last stage: tempering. This is the part of the process that gives the chocolate its shine and snap, as I learned in the hacienda kitchen with Linny. It also prevents bloom, which is when the butter and solids separate and the chocolate develops an uneven colour. Bloom doesn't necessarily mean that the chocolate is bad, but it's not very attractive. However,

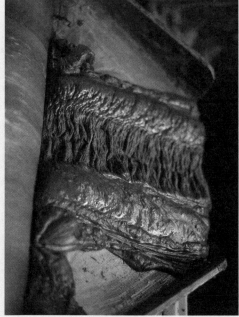

when you break open the big kilo bars of cacao or chocolate, sometimes you'll see a light colour in the centre: it's unavoidable.

When you temper the cacao and it goes into the mould, it gives off heat as it cools. It's important to get this heat out quickly, either through air-conditioning or a cooling tunnel. It shrinks a little as it cools, which allows it to come easily out of the mould.

My tempering machine is the only modern piece of equipment in the factory, so you'd think there would be fewer problems with it, wouldn't you? No such luck: I went through two machines before I found one that worked properly.

It didn't help to have a documentary team trailing me, filming *Willie's Wonky Chocolate Factory* for Channel 4, although eventually I got used to being filmed. When my new grinder arrived and I dropped it off the forklift truck, I totally forgot about the cameras. They were there in front of me, documenting every last bit of shock and dismay on my face, but I was completely oblivious to them. All I could think about was how disastrous it was to break the grinder: I just couldn't believe it had happened. However, I didn't have any time to waste; after a few moments of horrified disbelief, I decided that there was no use crying over spilt milk. I just had to get on and deal with it.

You can't imagine how much happiness was in the air the day a steady

stream of chocolate finally filled up the moulds in the tempering room. It was a truly wonderful sight to see tray upon tray stack up with cylindrical bars of beautiful balanced cacao, a far cry from the night when we moulded two thousand bars and they almost all bloomed. At last I was up and running. The thudding hum and thrum of the whole production line was music to my ears.

My next challenge was to find outlets that would sell my cacao. A few months before this, I had visited several shops and supermarkets to spread the word about what I was doing. I met with buyers and evangelised passionately about the wonders of using 100 per cent cacao as an ingredient in cooking.

It helped that there was going to be a documentary coming out, but I think people would have found my enthusiasm contagious no matter what. I was so excited that I couldn't help being explosively effusive when I talked about the farm, the harvest and the cacao. I felt incredibly lucky that I was selling something I believed in. It was the real McCoy and the flavour was my ammunition: my truffles and Cloud Forest Chocolate Cake bowled people over every time. Various potential stockists expressed an interest and told me to let them know when I'd reached the point of having a finished product.

My very first order came from a big London department store food hall – for 3,000 cacao bars. I jumped for joy when I heard the news. My first big order! After all the stress of the previous months – all that crushing anxiety about machines and bean supply – to get an order like that was like a gift from heaven! My dreams were beginning to come true at last. Venezuelan Black was finally going on sale.

Next I needed to expand quickly to keep up with overheads, which meant rapidly introducing the wider public to the idea of 100 per cent cacao as an ingredient. It was great that some of Marco Pierre White's chefs were using it in his restaurants, especially with savoury dishes like venison with chocolate, because this would have a direct influence on people's ideas about cacao and cooking.

I went on to do truffle tastings at farmers' markets and recipe demonstrations at food fairs. I also give talks about life as a cacao grower and manufacturer to all kinds of different special interest groups. I really enjoy this side of my work – I never grow tired of talking about cacao and how fantastic it is.

When the first episode of *Willie's Wonky Chocolate Factory* was aired, Tania's sister and her husband threw a party for us at their house in London. My family was there, along with the many friends who have supported us through the highs and lows of living on the farm and getting the factory off the ground.

Tania had already seen the first episode at a preview screening, but I hadn't

been able to bring myself to watch it up until then. My excuse was that I was so busy at the factory that I couldn't really spare the time to go to London to see it, but in fact I was dreading seeing myself on the TV. I needn't have worried, but no one can blame me for being a bit anxious beforehand. A few months later, I agreed to make another series.

People often ask whether I was nervous about failing. It's true that a lot went wrong along the way, but I never once thought that I wouldn't get there in the end. Luckily I was able to detach myself from the problems and focus on how to solve them. I always had confidence in my product and what I was trying to do.

I will go on doing a one hundred-hour week as long as I need to, even though it's exhausting. You've got to put 100 per cent into getting your business off the ground. The way I see it, you only get one shot at it and it would be mad to waste it. It frustrates me that I don't get to spend enough time at home, but it won't be forever. You can't relax until the business has a really solid base.

I've got lots of plans for the future. I'm still determined to revolutionise the way we see chocolate in this country and although I'm not there yet, I feel I might be getting there, slowly but surely.

Willie's Supreme Cacao is all about the different flavours of cacao, so when I came across an amazing Peruvian San Martin bean with tropical fruit liqueur flavour notes, I immediately wanted to add it to the family. I'm now producing Peruvian Black as well as Venezuelan Black, and maybe I'll go on to add other beans.

Cacao is such a wonderful product to work with. For a start, it's absolutely delicious. It works as a sweet and it's a wonderful, versatile, enriching cooking ingredient. It's also an endorphine and dopamine stimulant that enhances mood, alertness and concentration, boosts energy, reduces pain sensitivity, works as an antioxidant and contains vitamins and minerals! How could anyone possibly resist?

Willie's Rambunctious GET-UP & GOCOA!, my hot chocolate, is my next offering; then I want to produce Willie's Delectable Cacao – a sweetened dark chocolate bar that's really packed with flavour. After that, who knows? I've got a million ideas.

By the way, did you know that the botanical name for the cacao tree is *Theobroma cacao* – and *theobroma* means 'food of the gods'?

Viva cacao! It's everyone's affordable luxury. It tastes wonderful, it's great in food, it's good for you and it makes you feel absolutely fantastic.

Cooking with Cacao

Cacao adds richness and depth to many dishes, savoury and sweet.
It's excitingly versatile, offering different flavour profiles in different dishes.
The robust flavour notes, which survive at higher cooking temperatures, are
great for casseroles and other savoury dishes, while the subtle, fruity notes shine
through in a simple sauce or a mousse. The trick in savoury dishes is to use it as
a condiment, and how much you use depends to a degree on personal taste, as
with salt and pepper. It's incredibly easy too: just stir the grated cacao into the
dish (or as described in the recipes).

For sweet dishes, such as a truffle or a mousse, where you are looking for
the fine, fruity flavour notes, you need a more delicate approach, which is one
reason why the cacao for a sweet dish is usually melted in a bain-marie: a bowl
set over a saucepan of simmering water. Another reason is that cacao on its
own can catch and burn if put in a pan over direct heat.

Three ways to grate or crumble a bar of Willie's Cacao

1. Grate by hand on the coarse side of a kitchen grater.

2. Put a chunk in the food processor on carrot-grater mode.

3. Place the cacao on a chopping board and coarsely chop with a chef's
   knife. The cacao starts to flake away in chunks that are easily melted.

NB:

* Cacao will melt the moment it touches anything above body
  temperature, so you don't need to grate it too finely.

* There's no need to store it in the fridge; it just makes your job harder.

Cacao nibs

Sometimes a recipe calls for cacao nibs: this is the cacao after it's been fermented, roasted and winnowed, but before it's been ground, refined and conched. You can buy cacao nibs from specialist retailers or online; they are often sold under their French name, *grue de cacao*.

Substituting other chocolates

When you use 100% cacao, you get the full flavour of the bean, with nothing added and nothing taken away. If you can't get 100% cacao, experiment with other high-percentage chocolates. Try 85% for savoury dishes. In the sweet dishes, experiment with the 70% chocolates: use more 70% chocolate than you would 100% cacao, and reduce other ingredients, especially sugar and cream or butter, accordingly.

Stockists of Willie's cacao are listed on the website:
www.williescacao.com.

Cook's Notes

- All eggs are medium and free-range.

- 1 tsp is the equivalent of 5ml

- 1 tbsp is the equivalent of 15ml

My oven is fan-assisted, and so all temperatures in this book refer to a fan-assisted oven. For those of you with conventional ovens, I have given a guide below. You can simply add 20 degrees to the temperature I give you in the recipes. However, all ovens vary and it will not take long for you to get to know your own oven.

Willie's Fan Oven	Conventional Oven	Fahrenheit	Gas Mark
120 C	140 C	275 F	1
130 C	150 C	300 F	2
150 C	170 C	325 F	3
160 C	180 C	350 F	4
170 C	190 C	375 F	5
180 C	200 C	400 F	6
200 C	220 C	425 F	7
210 C	230 C	450 F	8

Get Up and Go

Get up and go-coa. Food of the Gods, fit for Kings and
drunk by all of us: a potent pick-me-up with health-
and energy-giving properties. Not for the weak.

This is the all-time get-up & go-coa! In Venezuela, it always worked to have a shot of it in the morning, when it was too early to eat. Then we'd take a thermos flask up the mountain on our way to see the howler monkeys and collect bananas from the cloud forest. A powerful, vitamin-rich antioxidant, it would keep us going all day. It gives you cacao's equivalent of caffeine – theobromine – and a real sense of wellbeing.

Venezuelan Hot Chocolate

(Serves 2)

25g cacao, finely grated
100ml water
Honey or sugar, to taste

Tip the cacao and water into a small pan and bring to the boil, stirring frequently. When thick and well combined, remove the hot chocolate from the heat. Add honey or sugar to taste. You can thin the hot chocolate by adding extra water or vary it by adding a splash of milk or rum, or try the variations overleaf.

Hot chocolate can be served in a variety of different ways, so it's easy to be imaginative and invent your own house special. The alcoholic hotties are great for cosying up with at home, or as a dessert at the end of a dinner party, served with a ginger biscuit. Fiery and delicious.

Tania's Hot Chocolate Variations

Spiced hot choc:
with ground nutmeg * ground cinnamon * cloves

Hot choc chilli shot:
with a whole chilli or some dried chilli flakes – remove before serving

Chococchino:
with hot frothed milk and a little extra grated cacao on top

Espresso choc shot:
½ espresso and ½ hot choc

Alcoholic hotties:
with rum * brandy * cognac * Baileys * or Cointreau. Serve in a shot glass and dress with small dots of fresh cream on the surface, using a teat pipette or a cocktail stick.

This is a real breakfast treat and a great way to kick-start your morning. As always, the chilli plays beautifully on the cacao: it's simply a great combination. Serve with toast.

Huevos Rancheros

(Serves 2)

1 tbsp olive oil
1 onion, finely chopped
1 garlic clove, crushed
1 red chilli (with or without seeds, according to taste)
1 red pepper, seeds removed, finely chopped
50g chorizo, thinly sliced
½ tsp dried oregano
2 large ripe tomatoes, roughly chopped, or 400g tin chopped tomatoes
2 eggs
2 tsp finely grated cacao

Heat the oil in a medium frying pan. Add the onion, garlic, chilli, red pepper, chorizo and oregano and fry over a medium heat for about 5 minutes or until soft.

Add the tomatoes and cook for a further 5 minutes, stirring occasionally. Season with salt and black pepper, then make 2 hollows in the mixture. Break an egg into each, cover and cook for another 3–5 minutes or until the eggs are set. Finish with a scattering of cacao.

Tania puts cacao nibs in her muesli every morning. They add a refreshing sharp flavour and they're packed with goodness. So here's a delicious, healthy start to the day...

Cacao Nib Muesli

(Makes 4–6 servings)

200g porridge oats
50g cacao nibs
50g hazelnuts, lightly crushed
50g flaked almonds
150g mixed dried fruit, such as sultanas, apricots, figs, goji berries, blueberries, cranberries and apples, roughly chopped

Preheat the oven to 160°C (fan).

Place the oats, cacao nibs, hazelnuts and almonds on a large baking tray and toast in the oven for 8–10 minutes, shaking regularly. Leave to cool.

Mix the toasted ingredients with the dried fruit. Keep in an airtight container if not used all at once.

I always surprise my friends with my Venezuelan breakfast: eggs fried in chilli oil with a light grating of cacao. The idea raises eyebrows, but everyone agrees it's delicious. It's a great way to convert non-believers. Annabel, Ricardo's wife, was the queen of arepas: flatbreads made with maize. I ran the farm in a very inclusive way, and cooking breakfast together was part of that ethic. We'd eat around 10.30am, after we'd done a few hours' work. We split the cooking – Annabel made the arepas and I made the beans. It was like two continents meeting in the kitchen, exchanging culinary tips. Back in Devon, with no Annabel to make the arepas, we eat toast instead, with avocado on the side to remind us of the farm.

Willie's Venezuelan Breakfast

(Serves 6 hungry people)

For the black beans:

4 tbsp olive oil

2 onions, diced

3 garlic cloves, finely chopped

2 red peppers, seeds removed, finely chopped

300g soaked and briefly boiled black beans (see introduction)

About 300ml chicken stock

2–3 tbsp grated cacao

To serve:

Chilli oil (to make your own, steep dried chillies in sunflower or olive oil), for frying

12 eggs

12 slices brown bread

2 or 3 ripe avocados

4 tbsp grated cacao

3 large ripe tomatoes, sliced

To prepare the beans, heat the olive oil in a large pan over a medium heat. Add the onions, garlic and peppers and fry until soft. Tip in the black beans and pour over enough chicken stock to cover. Simmer for 1 ½–2 hours or until soft. Stir in the cacao and season with salt and black pepper. (It's important, when cooking beans, to add salt only at the end.)

When you and your breakfast guests are ready to eat, heat a little chilli oil in a frying pan and fry the eggs. Toast the bread and, if necessary, reheat the beans. Halve the avocados, remove the stones, then peel and slice the flesh. Serve the fried eggs on the hot toast on individual plates, grating a little cacao over the top, with a couple of spoonfuls of black beans and several slices of avocado and tomato on the side.

Willie's Tip: If you use dried beans, as I always prefer to, soak them overnight, then drain them, cover with fresh water and bring to the boil. Boil for 3–5 minutes, then drain again, and they are ready to cook with. About 125g dried beans makes the 300g you need. I always prepare more and keep them in the fridge for the next few days' breakfasts.

Churros are the classic Venezuelan street food, served in the late afternoon and evening on every promenade, pavement and seafront walk. They are basically skinny South American doughnuts, sold in some places with hot chocolate for breakfast. The best churros we ever tasted were in the high Andes, in a square where they sold churros in one corner and fried pig's ears in the other. What a combination!

Churros

(Makes about 16)

150ml whole milk
150ml water
100g plain flour, sifted
Sunflower oil, for deep-frying
1 egg, beaten
Golden caster sugar and ground cinnamon, to serve

Pour the milk and water into a medium pan and bring to the boil. Add the flour and beat with a wooden spoon until smooth. Leave to cool slightly. Heat the oil in a deep-fat fryer or a large deep pan until it reaches 190°C. Gradually beat the egg into the dough until it is stiff and glossy. Transfer to a piping bag fitted with a large star nozzle.

Squeeze 10cm lengths of the mixture into the hot oil. Deep-fry for 3–5 minutes or until crisp and golden brown. Lift the churros out with tongs or a slotted spoon and lay on kitchen paper to drain.

Scatter over a little caster sugar and cinnamon and serve.

Willie's Tip: It's important not to heat the oil over 190°C or the exterior will brown too quickly and the interior remain uncooked. Also, sift the flour to get rid of clumps that can get trapped in the dough and cause the churros to have a blow-out. Use a star nozzle to get the classic churros shape.

Bloody Mary is a meal in itself. It's like an orchestra of ingredients and the cacao is the trombone. Don't forget your Tabasco.
Viva Sangre Maria!

Bloody Mary

For the cacao vodka:
100g cacao nibs, roasted
1 bottle of vodka

For a Bloody Mary:
45ml cacao vodka
90ml tomato juice
15ml lemon juice
Worcestershire sauce, to taste
Tabasco, to taste
Cacao, finely grated, to taste
Lemon wedge and stick of celery, to garnish

Prepare the cacao-infused vodka by adding the cacao nibs to the bottle of vodka. (You may have to discard or drink some of the vodka to get the nibs in comfortably.) Replace the lid and leave to infuse for at least 48 hours.

Make the Bloody Mary by placing a couple of ice cubes in the base of a highball glass. Strain the vodka into the glass. Stir in the tomato juice and lemon juice. Add Worcestershire sauce, Tabasco, cacao, and salt and black pepper to taste. Garnish with a lemon wedge and celery stick.

Enough of cakes, let them eat cacao bread! It's at its finest toasted.

Cacao Bread

(Makes 1 loaf)

200g strong white flour, plus extra for dusting
300g plain wholemeal flour
2 tsp salt
7g sachet fast-action dried yeast
50g cacao, finely grated
450ml warm water

Mix the flours, salt and yeast in a large bowl. Make a well in the centre. Stir the cacao into the water until completely dissolved, then pour the water and cacao mixture into the well and stir to incorporate all the dry ingredients. (If the dough seems a little stiff, add another tablespoon or two of water.) Tip on to a lightly floured work surface and knead the dough for 5–10 minutes until smooth. Place it in a lightly oiled bowl and leave to rise for 1 ½ hours or until doubled in size.

Grease a large loaf tin. Knock back the dough, then gently mould the dough into a loaf-shape. Place it in the tin and leave to prove for a further hour or until doubled in size.

Preheat the oven to 180°C (fan). Bake for 40 minutes until golden brown and the loaf sounds hollow when tapped underneath. Cool on a wire rack.

Another classic Venezuelan snack, often sold at the side of the road. Quick, filling and tasty, its pancake-style is a big hit with the kids. It can be topped with cheese or ham, syrup or jam. Little or large, savoury or sweet; it's up to you. I like them with slices of mozzarella or spread with cream cheese.

Cachapas (Chocolate Corn Cakes)

(Makes about 12)

4 corn on the cob
50ml cream
30g cacao, grated
25g butter

Slice the corn kernels away from the cobs. Put the kernels and the cream in a food processor and blitz to a paste. Add the cacao and give the mixture another quick blitz. Season well with salt and black pepper.

Melt the butter in a frying pan over a medium heat. Add spoonfuls of the mixture to the pan and gently flatten into rounds of 5–6cm. Fry for a few minutes, turning over halfway through, until golden on both sides.

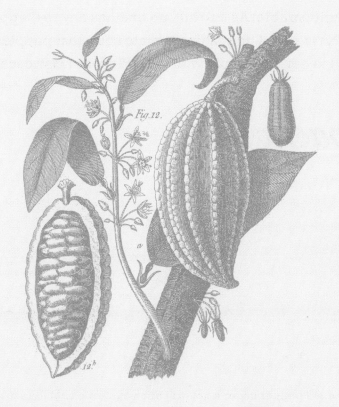

Lunches and Dinners

Cacao really is an incredible condiment – I liken
it to salt – it's the most exciting ingredient
made available for years.

In the rainy season, the humidity in Choroni can reach levels that are almost unbearable. As a result, no one has any real appetite, but gazpacho is a cool, refreshing tomato soup that people will always want to eat, especially with the El Tesoro twist: cacao.

Gazpacho

(Serves 4)

1 large red pepper, halved, seeds removed
1kg very ripe tomatoes
½ onion, diced
2 garlic cloves, finely chopped
½ large cucumber, peeled, seeds removed, chopped
150ml extra virgin olive oil
3 tbsp white wine vinegar
3 tbsp caster sugar
3 tbsp finely grated cacao

Roast the red pepper under a hot grill or on a griddle until the skin has blackened slightly. Allow to cool, then peel it. (Putting roasted peppers in a brown paper bag and leaving them to steam and cool can make them easier to peel.) Blanch the tomatoes in hot water for 10 seconds, then refresh them in cold water. Peel, seed and roughly chop. Place the pepper, tomatoes, onion, garlic and cucumber in a food processor and begin to blitz. While the processor is going, pour in the olive oil. Blitz the gazpacho until smooth.

Combine the vinegar and sugar in a small pan and heat until the sugar has dissolved. Stir in the cacao and continue to heat until the cacao has melted. Remove the pan from the heat and leave to cool slightly.

Stir the cacao syrup into the gazpacho. Season with salt and black pepper. Chill before serving.

Butternut squash is one of the simplest and tastiest soups to make.
Sweet and beautifully rich in colour, it's fundamentally easy to
prepare, and the slight sharpness of the cacao nibs contrasts well
with the sweetness of the squash.

Pumpkin & Red Pepper
Soup with Cacao Cream

(Serves 8)

2kg butternut pumpkin, deseeded,
  peeled, coarsely chopped
2 tbsp fresh rosemary, finely chopped
80ml extra virgin olive oil
2 red peppers, halved,
  seeds removed

2 large onions, roughly chopped
4 garlic cloves, crushed
1 litre vegetable or chicken stock
50g cacao, finely grated
Crème fraiche, to finish
Cacao nibs, to finish

Preheat the oven to 220°C (fan). Place the pumpkin in a large roasting tray.
Top with the rosemary and drizzle over half the oil. Season with salt and black
pepper then roast for 30 minutes or until tender. Halfway through, add the
pepper halves, cut-side down on a lightly oiled roasting tray.

Meanwhile, heat the remaining oil in a large saucepan over a medium heat.
Add the onion and garlic and fry until soft.

Take the pumpkin and peppers from the oven. Put the roasted peppers in a
brown paper bag and leave to steam and cool; this makes it easier to peel
them. Add the pumpkin to the onion and garlic, with enough of the stock to
cover. Bring to the boil. Reduce heat to low, cover and simmer for 10 minutes,
stirring occasionally.

Peel and chop the peppers and add to the soup. Pour the soup into a blender
and blitz until smooth. Adjust the seasoning if necessary and stir in the cacao.
Ladle the soup into bowls and finish with a spoon of crème fraiche and a
scattering of cacao nibs.

Sancocho is the soup – fish or meat – prepared by a big group of friends congregating by a river or on the beach. It is always shared with every passing soul. The point where I cross the river into our farm happens to be one of the favourite local spots for a weekend sancocho. The words, 'Epa, Willie, ven aqui! Sancocho!' were always music to my ears. In all my years in Venezuela, every single sancocho I've tried has been delicious. The secret is in gentle cooking and the liberal use of fresh herbs. No one is in a hurry. This is also excellent made with ribs of beef.

Sancocho Soup

(Serves 6)

2 tbsp olive oil

1 large onion, roughly chopped

4 garlic cloves, sliced

1.5kg organic free-range chicken, roughly chopped into 10 pieces

150g dried cannellini beans, soaked overnight, then drained

2 sweet potatoes, peeled and sliced

2 leeks, halved and sliced

4 carrots, halved and sliced

2 corn on the cob, sliced into 6 pieces each

4 tomatoes, roughly chopped

2 tbsp tomato purée

25g cacao, finely grated

Large handful of fresh coriander, chopped

Put the olive oil in a large saucepan and fry the onion and garlic over a medium-high heat until soft. Add the chicken pieces and sear well on all sides. Cover with water, tip in the drained, soaked beans and bring to the boil. Boil for 3–5 minutes, then reduce the heat and let simmer for 15 minutes. Add the sweet potatoes and cook for 40 minutes.

Add all the remaining ingredients, including half the coriander, and cook until the carrots are the required level of al dente. Serve with the remaining coriander sprinkled over the top.

Caponata should be sweet, sour and juicy – like this. It is best left overnight to allow the flavours to infuse. Serve at room temperature as an appetiser with some warm flatbread, or as an accompaniment to fish or meat.

Caponata

(Serves 4)

6 tbsp olive oil
2 aubergines, cut into cubes of about 1.5cm
1 red onion, finely sliced
3 sticks celery, finely sliced
6 plum tomatoes, peeled and seeds removed, roughly chopped
2 tbsp salted capers, rinsed and drained
10 green olives, pitted and roughly chopped
2 tbsp pine nuts
3 tbsp red wine vinegar
1½ tbsp caster sugar
1 tbsp finely grated cacao
Fresh basil leaves, to garnish

Heat 4 tablespoons of the olive oil in a large, heavy-based pan. Add the aubergines and cook until softened and lightly browned (you might have to do this in 2 batches). Remove from the pan and set aside.

Add the rest of the olive oil to the pan and sauté the onion and celery for a few minutes until soft.

Return the aubergine to the pan along with the tomatoes, capers, olives and pine nuts. Add the vinegar and sugar and season with salt and black pepper. Simmer for 20 minutes to allow the tomatoes to soften into the mixture. Stir in the grated cacao and cook for another 5 minutes. Sprinkle with basil leaves before serving.

Fresh squid weren't that easy to come by in Choroni; you could only get them on a first-come, first-served basis at the port in Puerto Colombia. There is nothing as tender as squid that are only a few hours old. With the colours still brilliant, they're like jewels from the sea.

Cacao Salt & Pepper Squid

Serves 4 (as a starter)

500g squid, cleaned
1 tsp black peppercorns
1 tsp dried chilli flakes
1 tsp sea salt
1 tsp finely grated cacao
1–2 tbsp olive oil
Lemon wedges and fresh coriander, to garnish

Cut the tentacles off the squid and set aside. Open out the squid tubes and lightly score with a crisscross pattern. Pat dry with kitchen paper, wrap in cling film and store in the refrigerator until ready to cook.

Place the peppercorns, chilli flakes and salt in a dry pan and toast over a medium heat until fragrant. Grind using a pestle and mortar. Stir in the cacao. Preheat a griddle pan over a high heat.

Remove the squid from the refrigerator. Drizzle over the oil, then dust with the cacao-spice mix.

Grill for 1–2 minutes – larger ones for 1 minute each side; small ones for 1 minute on one side only – or until the edges of the squid curl up. Serve with a garnish of lemon wedges and coriander.

Mole is an authentic Mexican dish with its roots in Aztec cuisine, whose sauce is based on the flavours of a selection of chillies and cacao.

Chicken Mole

(Serves 4–6)

5cm cinnamon stick

5 cloves

5 star anise

50g raw peanuts

3 tbsp olive oil

2 onions, roughly chopped

4 garlic cloves, chopped

6 chicken thighs

6 chicken legs

400g can plum tomatoes

3 ancho chillies, seeds removed

3 pasilla chillies, seeds removed

3 mulato chillies, seeds removed

90g cacao, finely grated

Chicken stock, to cover

50g tortilla chips

Preheat the oven to 200°C (fan). Dry-roast the spices and peanuts for 6–8 minutes. (This can also be done in a heavy-based pan on the stove.)

Meanwhile, heat the oil in a large casserole, add the onions and garlic and fry until soft.

Grind the toasted spices until fine (using a spice grinder or a pestle and mortar) and add them to the casserole. Stir in the peanuts. Tip the chicken into the casserole and fry on all sides until golden brown: about 5 minutes.

Add the tomatoes, chillies and cacao and enough chicken stock to cover. Cover and simmer for 30–35 minutes.

Remove the chicken from the mole and set aside. Stir in the tortilla chips, pour the sauce into a food processor and blitz until smooth. (The tortilla chips add a nice maize quality and help thicken the sauce.)

Return the sauce to the casserole. Add the chicken, cover and simmer for a further 30 minutes. Serve with rice.

Willie's Tip: Mole is best eaten the following day.

This is a rich, smooth appetiser that doubles as a late-night snack. I'm renowned for my night snacking – once I woke up in front of the fridge to find a slice of toast and chicken liver pâté in my hand. Serve this with toasted brioche and cornichons.

Chocolate Chicken Liver Pâté

(Serves 4)

175g unsalted butter, softened
450g chicken livers, trimmed and cleaned
2 shallots, finely chopped
1 tsp fresh thyme leaves
2 garlic cloves, finely chopped
2 tbsp brandy
2 tsp finely grated cacao

Heat a tablespoon of the butter in a frying pan until foaming.

Add half the livers and fry quickly on both sides until golden, but still pink in the middle, about 4–5 minutes. Remove to a plate. Repeat with another tablespoon of butter and livers. Transfer the livers and pan juices to a food processor.

In the same pan, heat another tablespoon of butter. Add the shallots, thyme and garlic and fry over a moderate heat until the shallots are soft but not coloured.

Add the brandy and cacao and season with some black pepper. Scrape the pan to collect all the flavourful bits stuck to the base.

Tip everything into the food processor. Add the remaining butter. Blitz until very smooth. (If you're not serving the pâté immediately, top with clarified butter, and refrigerate.)

I like to keep my recipes simple, especially in summer. This is a barbecue quickie: a delicious piece of instant savoury-sweet gratification. The best bit is the crispy bit and it's all crispy bit!

Sticky Chocolate Ribs

(Serves 4)

6 tbsp tomato purée
2 tbsp harissa
2 tbsp grated cacao
2 tbsp sunflower oil
2 tsp honey
1kg pig ribs (8 ribs)

Put all the ingredients for coating the ribs into a small pan along with a pinch of salt. Place over a medium heat and stir occasionally until thick and glossy. Leave to cool slightly.

Pour the sauce over the ribs and turn the ribs over and over until coated. Cook the ribs over a medium barbecue for 20–30 minutes, depending on their size, turning them frequently and brushing regularly with the sauce.

All my vegetarian friends say, 'Yes, Will, but what do *we* do with cacao?' Risotto is the obvious option; it's a classic vegetarian dish. Porcini and cacao, both with distinct, strong flavours and rich, deep colours, make the perfect union.

Porcini & Chocolate Risotto

(Serves 4)

4–5 tbsp olive oil
1 onion, finely chopped
3 garlic cloves, finely chopped
100g dried porcini mushrooms
25g butter
250g arborio rice
1 litre hot chicken or vegetable stock
2 tbsp cacao, finely grated
Parmesan, to serve

Heat the olive oil in a large pan. Add the onion and garlic and fry over a gentle heat until soft.

Meanwhile, place the porcini mushrooms in a small bowl and cover with boiling water to rehydrate.

Drop the butter into the pan. Stir in the rice.

Add the porcini and the liquid they were soaked in. Simmer, stirring occasionally until the liquid has been absorbed. Add a ladleful of stock and simmer, stirring again, until the liquid has been absorbed. Continue adding the stock in this way until all the liquid has been absorbed and the rice is plump and tender.

Stir in the cacao to finish. Season with salt and black pepper and serve with grated Parmesan.

Look for ripe vine tomatoes for this lovely salad – it makes a difference. This makes more dressing than you need; keep the rest for another salad.

Puy Lentil & Roast Tomato Salad

(Serves 4)

250g small vine tomatoes, halved
Olive oil, to drizzle
200g Puy lentils
200g French beans or string beans, topped and tailed
½ garlic clove, crushed
5 tbsp cacao dressing
Handful of fresh flat-leaf parsley leaves

For the cacao dressing:
2 tbsp sherry vinegar
1 tbsp finely grated cacao
6 tbsp extra virgin olive oil

To make the dressing, warm the sherry vinegar in a small pan and add the grated cacao. Mix until the cacao dissolves into the vinegar. Pour into a small bowl, season with salt and black pepper, then whisk in the oil. Set aside until ready to use.

Preheat the oven to 200°C (fan). Put the tomatoes, cut-sides up, on a small baking tray. Drizzle with a little olive oil and season with salt and black pepper. Roast for 15–20 minutes or until slightly browned but still firm.

Meanwhile, put the lentils in a pan, cover with cold water, bring to the boil then simmer for 15–20 minutes until just tender. Blanch the beans in a pan of boiling, salted water for 3 minutes until just tender, then refresh under cold water to hold their colour.

Drain the lentils, then toss with the garlic and cacao dressing. Season.

Fold the beans and parsley and most of the roasted tomatoes through the lentils. Garnish the top of the salad with the remaining tomato halves, and serve.

I first learned to prepare coconut milk in Thailand in the late 1980s. Like most things, homemade is best. My memories are of older women chewing betel nut and grating coconut by hand, then massaging the mass in water for ten or fifteen minutes until all the flavour had come out. When Tania and I were living on the beach at Cepe, I taught this same method to the local mamas. When you live on the beach, the coconut is king, whether you're burning the husk to keep the flies away in the evening and the shell to fuel the barbecue, or using the coconut for piña coladas or coconut milk, or bronzing your body with the oil.

Fish Curry with Coconut & Cacao

(Serves 4)

2 tbsp olive oil
1 onion, finely chopped
3 garlic cloves, finely chopped
1 chipotle chilli (with or without seeds, according to taste)
1 tbsp coriander seeds

1 tbsp cumin seeds
1 tbsp cacao nibs
300ml coconut cream
4 white fish fillets or steaks, such as cod, haddock or hake

Heat the olive oil in a medium frying pan. Add the onion, garlic and chilli and fry until soft.

Tip the spices and cacao nibs into a small frying pan and dry-fry for 30 seconds over a medium heat. Grind the toasted spices and nibs using a pestle and mortar, then stir them into the onion and garlic mixture. Fry for 2 minutes.

Pour in the coconut cream and add the fish. Simmer for 10–12 minutes. Season with salt and black pepper and serve.

I once catered for a wedding and the client said, 'My boys are only eighteen and I'm worried about them getting drunk, so I want something that will really fill them up.' So I served them braised lamb shanks with mashed potato and every plate came back with just the bone. It's a hearty, tender, tasty meal, fit for your boy or Henry VIII!

Braised Lamb Shanks

(Serves 4)

3 tbsp olive oil
4 lamb shanks
1 large onion, finely chopped
3 garlic cloves, sliced
2 sticks celery, finely chopped
Few sprigs of fresh rosemary

2 bay leaves
1 tbsp tomato purée
400g can tomatoes
½ bottle white wine
500ml chicken or lamb stock
50g cacao, finely grated

Preheat the oven to 180°C (fan).

Heat the oil in a large, ovenproof casserole on the hob and brown off the lamb shanks.

Remove the shanks from the casserole and set aside. Turn down the heat, add the onion, garlic and celery and fry for 3–5 minutes or until soft.

Add the herbs and stir in the tomato purée and tomatoes. Season well with salt and black pepper.

Return the shanks to the casserole, then pour in the wine and stock. Bring to a simmer, then cover and place in the oven for 1½-2 hours or until the lamb is tender.

Remove the lamb and leave to rest. Place the casserole over a medium heat and cook until the sauce is reduced by half. Stir in the cacao. Serve the shanks and sauce with mashed potato.

I fed around half a dozen of my friends for about five years on spaghetti bolognese. When I cook it for my kids, I always ask them, 'How's the spaghetti bolognese?' and they always reply, 'You put chocolate in it again, Daddy! It's lovely.'

Spaghetti Bolognese

(Serves 4)

2 tbsp olive oil
2 large onions, finely chopped
3 garlic cloves, crushed
1 large carrot, finely chopped
500g minced beef
300ml red wine
2 x 400g cans plum tomatoes, crushed
250ml concentrated chicken stock

3 bay leaves
1 heaped tsp dried oregano
1 heaped tsp dried thyme
50g cacao, finely grated
Handful of fresh basil leaves, torn
400g dried spaghetti
Freshly grated Parmesan cheese, to serve

Heat the oil in a large saucepan over a medium heat. Add the onions, garlic and carrot and fry until soft. Increase the heat and add the minced beef. Fry until browned all over.

Pour in the wine and boil until it has reduced in volume by about a third. Reduce the heat and stir in the tomatoes, stock, bay leaves, oregano and thyme. Stir in the cacao.

Cover and simmer over a gentle heat for 1–1½ hours until rich and thick, stirring occasionally. At the end of the cooking time, stir in the basil and season well with salt and black pepper. (When making bolognese sauce, it's important to add the salt only at the end.)

Meanwhile, bring a large pan of salted water to the boil and cook the spaghetti according to the packet instructions. Drain and divide between warmed plates. Top with the bolognese sauce and finish with a scattering of Parmesan cheese.

This is a great summer buffet dish. You can serve it hot, but if there are any latecomers, it's just as good cold.

Chicken Breasts
with Red Pepper & Cacao Stuffing

(Serves 4)

4 chicken breast fillets, skin on
1 tbsp olive oil, plus a little extra
1 small onion, finely chopped
1 red pepper, seeds removed, chopped
Pinch of dried chilli flakes
4 pitted black olives, chopped
½ tbsp finely grated cacao
Small handful of fresh oregano leaves, chopped

Create a pocket for the stuffing by sliding your finger between the chicken skin and the breast. Set the chicken aside.

Heat 1 tablespoon of the oil in a frying pan and add the onion, pepper and chilli flakes. Fry until soft. Stir in the olives and cacao. Season with salt and black pepper, then tip into a food processor and blitz until smooth. Divide the mixture between the chicken breasts, carefully pushing it into the pockets created. Scatter over the oregano leaves and drizzle with a little extra olive oil.

Heat a large frying pan with the remaining oil over a medium heat. Place the stuffed chicken breasts in the pan, skin-side down. Fry for 25–30 minutes or until the skin is crisp and the breasts are cooked, turning once.

Willie's Tip: Before you start cooking, make sure no stuffing paste is exposed on the chicken breasts as it will burn. If any has seeped out, push it back under the skin.

I never got my head round conventional marinating. It always added a great flavour to the outside, but I wanted to get the flavour inside too. The result was one of my 'scientific moments', when I injected the cacao marinade into the meat using a large syringe. The combination of flavours works really well. I was inspired by the fact that the ginger grew in the shade of the cacao: they came together once again in the marinade.

Junkie Pig

(Serves 8)

500ml white wine
100ml balsamic vinegar
Garlic cloves from half a bulb, peeled
  and roughly chopped
10cm chunk of fresh ginger, peeled
  and roughly chopped
1 red chilli (with or without seeds,
  according to taste)

2 tbsp honey
25g cacao, finely grated
2 tbsp fennel seeds
2 tbsp sea salt
2.5kg boned and rolled pork
  shoulder, skin deeply scored

Preheat the oven to 220°C (fan).

Prepare the marinade by pouring the wine and balsamic vinegar into a small pan. Boil until reduced by half. Add the garlic, ginger, chilli and honey and simmer for 15 minutes. Remove the pan from the heat and strain the mixture, discarding the garlic, ginger and chilli. Stir in the cacao until melted.

Grind the fennel seeds and sea salt in a pestle and mortar.

Lift the pork shoulder into a roasting tin and push the fennel and sea salt into the slits in the pork skin.

Load the marinade into a syringe with a large gauge and inject it at regular intervals all over the flesh of the pork.

Calculate the roasting time for the joint. Allow 1 hour 10 minutes for every kilogram. Roast the pork for 30 minutes or until the skin has turned golden and very crisp. Turn the oven temperature down to 170°C and roast for the remaining time. Rest for 10–15 minutes before carving and serving.

Willie's Tip: This method of marinating works so effectively because the syringe pushes the marinade deep into the flesh of the pork. If you don't have a syringe, use a turkey baster. You could leave the shoulder in the marinade overnight (avoid getting it on the skin) but it doesn't penetrate as much. Be sure to turn the pan juices into a gravy by adding a splash of wine, some stock and a touch more cacao.

Coq au Vin is one of my winter favourites. It's a hearty tasty meal, and with cacao added it's simply *rico*.

Coq au Vin

(Serves 4)

1 whole organic free-range
chicken, about 1.5kg
2 onions
1 carrot
1 stick celery
2 bouquet garni
75g butter

2 tbsp olive oil
Garlic cloves from half a bulb, peeled
150g unsmoked back bacon,
roughly chopped
1 bottle red wine
1–2 tbsp finely grated cacao

Preheat the oven to 200°C (fan).

Remove the legs, wings and breast meat from the chicken. Place the chicken carcass in a roasting tin and roast for 30–40 minutes, or until golden brown. Transfer the carcass to a large pot. Add 1 onion, the carrot, celery and 1 bouquet garni. Cover with cold water and simmer for 35–40 minutes. Strain, discarding the vegetables and bones.

Season the chicken pieces with salt and black pepper. Heat the butter and oil in a large casserole. Add the chicken and fry until the skin is evenly browned. Meanwhile, blitz the remaining onion and the garlic cloves in a food processor until finely chopped. Remove the chicken from the casserole, add the onion and garlic, along with the bacon, and fry until soft and brown.

Turn the heat up and deglaze the casserole with a good splash of red wine. Return the chicken legs and wings to the pot. Pour in the remaining red wine and 150ml of stock. Add the remaining bouquet garni. Cook over a low heat for 1 hour, topping up the liquid if necessary with stock. Add the chicken breasts and cook for a further 20 minutes or until the chicken is cooked. Stir in the cacao to finish and serve with mashed potato.

Tagine is the mole of the Middle East, a classic dish that is thrown together using whatever meat you have in your fridge. Here, the strong flavours of saffron and cacao are softened by the sweetness of the dates. It's great on the day, and even better the next.

Lamb Tagine
with Dates & Chocolate

(Serves 4)

1kg lamb shoulder, cut into 12 pieces
2 onions, coarsely chopped
2 tsp ground ginger
1 tsp ground cinnamon
½ tsp saffron threads
2 tbsp whole skinned almonds
3 garlic cloves, chopped
25g cacao, finely grated
200g chopped tomatoes
1 litre chicken or vegetable stock
100g pitted dates

Put all the ingredients (except the dates) in a casserole, pouring over the stock and enough water to cover. Bring to the boil then simmer for 1½ hours with the lid on. Remove the lid, add the dates and simmer for a further 30 minutes (to reduce the sauce a little). Season to taste with salt and black pepper if necessary, and serve with couscous.

Cacao goes very well with game: the two strong flavours complement each other beautifully.

Pheasant & Cacao Casserole

(Serves 4)

2 pheasants
20g butter
2 large onions, chopped
2 carrots
2 sticks celery
1 large garlic clove
2 rashers streaky bacon
500ml red wine

300ml good chicken stock
3 juniper berries
1 clove
2 bay leaves
3 black peppercorns
Few sprigs of fresh thyme
Small piece orange peel
10g cacao, grated

Preheat the oven to 175°C/Gas 4.

Cut each pheasant into 4 pieces. Melt the butter in a casserole dish and brown the pheasant pieces lightly; you might have to do this in 2 batches. Remove the pheasant and add the chopped onions with a good pinch of salt. Cook for about 10 minutes until soft and brown, stirring occasionally.

Chop the carrots, celery, garlic and bacon, then add to the casserole and cook for a further 5 minutes. Add a good splash of wine to deglaze the casserole, scraping up any bits stuck on the base.

Return the pheasant pieces to the casserole along with the remainder of the wine and the chicken stock. Heat through, then add the juniper berries, clove, bay leaves, peppercorns, thyme and orange peel. Put the lid on and transfer to the oven for about 1¼ hours, or until the meat is cooked.

If you prefer an even richer, thicker sauce, pour off half the liquid into another pan and reduce briskly before returning to the casserole dish. Lastly add the grated cacao, stirring in thoroughly, tasting as you go. You might want to add a little more! For a touch of South America, add a teaspoon of mild chilli sauce with the stock.

Living in the country, game is cheap and cheerful. By the end of the season, it's game over: everybody's had it up to their ears. Here a little 'toquecito' of cacao makes the difference to a classic country dish.

Partridge Basted with Cacao

(Serves 8)

50g goose fat
4 tbsp finely grated cacao
2 tbsp olive oil
8 oven-ready partridges
24 slices pancetta
Few sprigs of fresh thyme

Preheat the oven to 200°C (fan).

Place the goose fat and cacao in a small pan and heat until the goose fat has melted, stirring occasionally. Remove the pan from the heat and leave to cool slightly.

Heat the olive oil in a large frying pan. Season the partridges with salt and black pepper then add them to the pan. Fry the birds until golden brown allover, then remove from the pan. Leave to cool slightly.

Use a pastry brush to paint the birds with the chocolate goose fat. Wrap 3 slices of pancetta around each partridge, sprinkle over the thyme, place in a roasting tray and roast for 25–30 minutes. Leave the birds to rest before serving with gravy (see page 168) and roast vegetables.

Willie's Tip: Game is often paired with chocolate in European cooking. This probably originated in Spain (echoing the use of it in Mexico) and was then taken up by the Italians, who add it to dishes containing wild boar.

If people are grating a little cacao into their gravy at Christmas time, I'll know I've succeeded. It is truly one of the great enrichers of flavour and the secret to a great gravy.

Chicken Cacao Gravy

(Makes 300ml)

2 organic or free-range chicken carcasses
2 carrots
2 sticks celery
1 large onion
250ml red wine
2 black peppercorns
2 bay leaves
Few sprigs of fresh thyme
2 litres of water
4 tsp grated cacao

Preheat the oven to 180°C (fan).

Roast the chicken carcasses for 1 hour. Remove from the oven and place in a large pan with the carrots, celery, onion, red wine, peppercorns, bay leaves, thyme and a pinch of salt. Add enough water to cover the ingredients, and simmer gently for 1 hour with the lid on.

Strain the stock and return to the heat. Discard the vegetables and bones, Reduce to 300ml by boiling fairly rapidly. Remove any fat from the surface. Add the grated cacao and stir until melted into the gravy.

This is adult ketchup with mountains of flavour that jumps out at you. It's great with meat, especially steak and sausages.

Tomato & Cacao Ketchup

(Makes 1 large or several small bottles)

3kg large ripe tomatoes
1 large onion, sliced
100g soft brown sugar
150ml cider vinegar
2 garlic cloves, crushed
1 tbsp tomato purée
¼ tsp mustard powder

¼ tsp allspice
¼ tsp ground mace
1 cinnamon stick
4 cloves
½ tsp black peppercorns
1 bay leaf
50g cacao, finely grated

Sterilise the bottle or bottles you want to use for the ketchup.

Cut a cross in the bottom of each tomato, then blanch in boiling water for about 30 seconds. Run the tomatoes under cold water and remove their skins. Roughly chop before placing in a medium pan along with the onion. Simmer, for 20–25 minutes, stirring occasionally.

Push the tomatoes through a fine sieve. Discard the pulp in the sieve and pass the tomatoes through the sieve a second time. Return to the pan and add the sugar, vinegar, garlic, tomato purée, mustard powder, allspice and mace. Tie the cinnamon, cloves, peppercorns and bay leaf in a piece of muslin to make a bouquet garni and add this to the pan.

Simmer the ketchup for about 45–50 minutes or until thick, stirring frequently. Remove the bouquet garni, season with salt and black pepper and stir in the cacao. Leave to cool, then pour into the bottle or bottles.

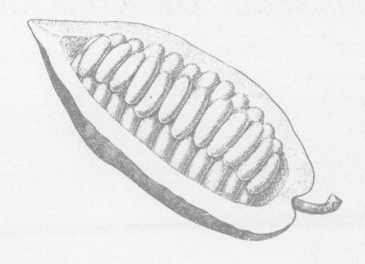

Confections:
Cakes, Puddings & Other Sweet Stuff

The rich intensity of cacao lends a wonderfully powerful
taste to any cake or pudding – the perfect way to
end any meal or even start the day.

I've taught all my friends how to make this cake. It's the king of cakes and simply sexy, the way to everyone's heart.

Cloud Forest Chocolate Cake

(Serves 12)

For the cake:
180g cacao, finely grated
250g unsalted butter
6 eggs
50g light muscovado sugar
125g golden caster sugar
100g ground almonds

For the icing:
250ml double cream
75g golden caster sugar
90g cacao, finely grated

Preheat the oven to 170°C (fan). Line a 25cm springform cake tin with baking paper.

For the cake, melt the cacao and butter by placing them in a heatproof bowl over a pan of simmering water.

Meanwhile, beat the eggs with the muscovado and caster sugar until pale and doubled in volume.

Stir the cacao mixture into the eggs. Fold in the ground almonds, then tip the cake mix into the prepared tin. Bake for 35 minutes, or until slightly but evenly risen all over and a knife inserted into the centre comes out clean. Leave to cool in the tin.

Prepare the icing by gently heating the cream and sugar until almost boiling. Remove from the heat then stir in the cacao until it has melted. Leave to cool then spread over the cake.

Willie's Tip: Dust with icing sugar or cocoa powder instead of the icing. Keep the cake at room temperature – it can go too solid if put in the fridge.

Kids love cooking and cupcakes are *it*. They can be made, cooked and decorated in minutes. Tania and the kids make the best cupcakes in the world. They are never sickly sweet, like other cupcakes can be, because they always use cacao instead of drinking chocolate, along with a darker sugar in smaller quantities than most recipes ask for.

Chocolate Cupcakes

(Makes 12)

50g cacao, finely grated
125g unsalted butter
125g golden caster sugar
2 large eggs
125g self-raising flour
2 tbsp whole milk

For the icing:
50ml water
20g golden caster sugar
20g cacao, finely grated

Preheat the oven to 200°C (fan). Arrange 12 paper cases on a baking tray or in a muffin tray.

Melt the cacao by placing it in a heatproof bowl set over a pan of simmering water.

Place the butter and sugar in a food processor and blitz until creamed. Add the eggs and blitz until combined.

Tip in the flour and blitz until the mixture is smooth. Stir in the cacao and milk.

Divide the mixture between the paper cases and bake for 15–20 minutes.

Leave the cupcakes to cool on a wire rack and prepare the icing. Tip the water and sugar into a small pan and boil until the sugar has dissolved. Stir in the cacao and continue to boil until well-combined. Transfer the icing to a bowl and place in the refrigerator until cool and firm. Spread over the cupcakes. Decorate as desired.

Tania keeps a production line of brownies going: her octopus tentacles reach far and wide, from primary and upper schools to riding stables and local fetes. She has bartered brownies for riding lessons and cacao for a kitchen table! Her brownies get her everywhere.

Brownies

(Makes 12)

250g cacao, finely grated
300g unsalted butter
6 whole eggs
2 egg yolks
300g golden caster sugar
80g plain flour, sifted

Preheat the oven to 180°C (fan). Grease and line a 20cm-square baking tin with non-stick baking paper.

Melt the cacao and butter by placing them in a heatproof bowl set over a pan of simmering water.

Meanwhile, whisk the eggs, egg yolks and sugar together until pale.

Stir the melted cacao and butter into the eggs. Fold in the flour and pour the mixture into the prepared tin. Bake for 25–30 minutes. Leave to cool in the tin.

Willie's Tip: You'll know when they are ready as the surface should be crisp and papery and the centre rich and gooey.

Everybody remembers eating flapjacks when they were young.
If they'd had a cacao farm, they would have added it too. It's great!

Chocolate Flapjacks

(Makes 12)

100g unsalted butter
100g light soft brown sugar
6 tbsp golden syrup
60g cacao, finely grated
300g porridge oats

Preheat the oven to 180°C (fan). Lightly grease a baking tin about 25 x 20cm.

Melt the butter with the sugar and golden syrup in a small pan over a
medium heat, stirring occasionally. Add the cacao and stir until melted
and well combined.

Remove from the heat and stir in the oats until completely coated in
the mixture. Spoon into the prepared tin, smooth the top and bake for
20–25 minutes until firm and dark golden.

Use a knife to mark out 12 pieces. Leave the flapjacks to cool in the tin.

This is one of the early classics that came from the El Tesoro kitchen. I taught it to many of the people who passed through the hacienda and it has now reached far and wide in the world! It's excellent for tasting the flavour notes of the cacao, due to the simplicity of its ingredients.

El Tesoro Mousse Cake

(Serves 12)

180g cacao, finely grated
250g unsalted butter
5 eggs
200g golden caster sugar
1 tsp vanilla extract

Preheat the oven to 160°C (fan). Line a 25cm cake tin with non-stick baking paper.

Melt the cacao and butter by placing them in a large heatproof bowl set over a pan of simmering water.

Meanwhile, beat the eggs with the sugar and the vanilla extract until pale yellow and fluffy.

Pour the cacao mixture into the eggs and beat to combine.

Stand the lined tin in a roasting tray and fill the tin with the mousse mixture. Pour enough boiling hot water into the roasting tray to come halfway up the side of the tin. Bake for 30 minutes or until set. Leave to cool in the tin.

Willie's Tip: In Venezuela – or anywhere hot and full of living things – the mousse cake would have to be kept in the fridge. Then, to turn it out, we'd run the dish over a gas flame or heat the sides with a blowtorch.

When I got back from Venezuela, I hadn't made a cheesecake in ages – you don't get much soft cheese in the tropics. I was trying cacao in everything at the time, so when I made my first cheesecake, I mixed in some of El Tesoro's finest. Soft cheese and cacao is a marriage made in heaven, as I quickly discovered.

Heavenly Cheesecake

(Serves 8)

100g digestive biscuits, finely crushed
30g oatcakes, finely crushed
1 tbsp ground almonds
50g unsalted butter
650g mixed soft cheeses, such as
   cream cheese and mascarpone
125g golden caster sugar

6 egg yolks
2 tsp vanilla extract
1 tsp cornflour
25g cacao, finely grated
200g mixed soft fruit, such as
   raspberries and blueberries

Preheat the oven to 120°C (fan). Line a 20cm springform cake tin with non-stick baking paper.

Combine the digestives, oatcakes and almonds.

Make a beurre noisette by heating the butter in a pan over a medium heat. When it stops sizzling and develops a nutty aroma, remove it from the heat immediately. Strain, discarding any dark solids left in the sieve. Stir the beurre noisette into the biscuit mix, then press into the bottom of the prepared tin. Place the tin in the refrigerator to chill and set.

Tip the cheeses, sugar, egg yolks, vanilla extract and cornflour into a food processor and blitz until smooth and creamy. Fold in the cacao.

Remove the tin from the refrigerator and cover the biscuit base with the cheese filling. Push the fruit down into the filling and smooth off the top. Bake for 1¼ hours. The cheesecake is ready when the edges have browned and the centre is just set.

When I was growing up, every house had a tin of biscuits, and El Tesoro was no different. There was always a box of chocolate biscuits on the go for our kids and their friends. They were so good that our daughter Sophia's first word was 'gagi', which was her way of saying *galleta*, the Spanish for biscuit. We sometimes added nutmeg, which grew on the trees on the lawn.

Chocolate Biscuits

(Makes 12)

150g cacao, finely grated
100g unsalted butter
150g golden caster sugar
1 tsp vanilla extract
1 egg, beaten
100g plain flour
1 tsp baking powder

Preheat the oven to 180°C (fan). Line a couple of baking trays with non-stick baking paper.

Melt the cacao by placing it in a heatproof bowl set over a pan of simmering water.

Meanwhile, beat the butter with the sugar, vanilla extract and egg in a bowl until smooth and combined. Stir in the melted cacao, then the flour and baking powder.

Place 12 spoonfuls of the mixture on to the prepared baking trays and bake for 12–15 minutes or until firm. Leave to cool on the trays.

Willie's Tip: This is a basic chocolate biscuit recipe that can be adapted by pushing nuts such as pecans – or hazelnuts or dried fruit like raisins or dates – into the surface of the biscuits just before baking.

Nuts and chocolate are always great together, whether you're
making marzipan or pecan pie.

Chocolate Pecan Tart

(Serves 8)

For the pastry:
200g plain flour
100g unsalted butter
100g golden caster sugar
2 egg yolks

For the filling:
180g cacao, finely grated
50g unsalted butter
75g golden caster sugar
175ml maple syrup
3 eggs
100g pecan nuts

Preheat the oven to 190°C (fan). Grease and flour a 23cm loose-bottomed flan tin.

To make the pastry, rub the flour and butter together (or whiz in a food
processor), then stir in the sugar. Add the egg yolks and mix until you have
a dough. (If the dough is dry, add a little water.) Knead briefly until smooth,
then wrap in cling film and chill in the refrigerator for at least 15 minutes.

Meanwhile, for the filling, melt the cacao and butter by placing them in a large
heatproof bowl over a pan of simmering water.

Put the sugar and maple syrup in a small pan and heat gently until the
sugar has dissolved. Leave to cool.

Whisk the eggs in a bowl then whisk in the chocolate and syrup mixtures.
Stir in the pecans.

Roll the pastry out on a lightly floured surface. Line the prepared tin with it.
Place a sheet of greaseproof paper over the pastry then cover with baking
beans. Bake blind for 10–15 minutes. Remove the paper and beans and return
the pastry to the oven for a couple of minutes if it's still slightly tacky. Pour the
filling into the pastry case and bake for 10–15 minutes or until the nuts have
browned and the filling is firm. Leave to cool slightly before serving.

Tiramisu means 'pick-me-up' in Italian, so with cacao it's a double pick-me-up!

Tiramisu

(Serves 8)

4 eggs, separated
100g golden caster sugar
2 tsp vanilla extract
500g mascarpone
300ml strong cold black coffee
4 tbsp amaretto or rum
24 Savoiardi or lady finger sponge biscuits
25g cacao, finely grated

Whisk the egg yolks, half the sugar and the vanilla extract together until pale yellow and fluffy. Stir in the mascarpone until smooth and creamy.

Beat the egg whites with the remaining sugar in a separate bowl with a pinch of salt until shiny and stiff.

Fold the egg whites into the mascarpone mixture.

Pour the coffee and liqueur into a dish and quickly dip the biscuits in it, one by one.

Arrange a layer of 12 of the moist biscuits in the base of a large rectangular serving dish. Spoon over half of the mascarpone mixture. Top with the remaining biscuits and finish with the rest of the mascarpone mixture. Cover and chill in the refrigerator until you're ready to serve. Just before serving, dust with the cacao.

Venezuela is a paradise for eating ice cream – and when it's hot and humid, there's nothing else like a really rich chocolate ice cream. This is so good it's beyond belief.

Deep, Dark & Delicious Ice Cream

(Makes about 1.5 litres)

900ml double cream
225ml whole milk
8 egg yolks
360g golden caster sugar
360g cacao, finely grated
2 tsp vanilla extract

Pour the cream and milk into a large pan and bring nearly to the boil over a gentle heat.

Whisk the egg yolks and sugar until pale.

Whisk a cupful of the hot cream mixture into the eggs and sugar.

Pour this custard mixture back into the pan and cook over a low heat for 8–10 minutes, stirring constantly until thick.

Remove the pan from the heat, stir in the cacao until melted, then stir in the vanilla extract. Cool, churn and freeze in an ice-cream maker. (If you don't have an ice-cream maker, tip the ice cream into a bowl, then put the bowl in the freezer until the ice cream starts to freeze around the edges. Stir well, then repeat the process twice more until the ice cream is smooth. Transfer to a sealable container for longer term storage.)

This is the all-time classic: a dynamite of a warm gooey pudding in portions that you don't have to share. It's also very easy to make. When it starts to split on the top, it's ready. Needs to be served straight from the oven.

Gooey Chocolate Puddings

(Makes 6–8)

180g cacao, finely grated
200g unsalted butter
175g golden caster sugar
6 eggs
2 tsp vanilla extract
40g ground almonds

Preheat the oven to 160°C (fan). Grease 6-8 ramekins.

Melt the cacao and butter by placing them, along with a 60g of the caster sugar, in a large heatproof bowl set over a pan of simmering water.

Meanwhile, lightly beat the eggs with the remaining caster sugar and the vanilla extract in a bowl.

Stir the ground almonds into the melted cacao and butter mixture.

Gradually fold the cacao mixture into the egg mixture. Divide the mixture between the ramekins and bake for 12–15 minutes. The tops will rise and start splitting when they are ready. Serve at once.

Willie's Tip: Try adding dried fruit soaked in alcohol (such as apricots in brandy or raisins in rum) for an adult twist.

You could only ever get Golden Delicious apples in Venezuela – and they're no good for baking. So I couldn't wait to buy cooking apples again when I got back to England. The autumn English orchard meets the cacao plantation in this classic country dish.

Baked Apples

(Serves 4)

4 large English cooking apples
50g dark muscovado sugar
50g hazelnuts, crushed
50g raisins
2 tbsp finely grated cacao
½ tsp ground cinnamon
Juice of 1 orange

Preheat the oven to 180°C (fan).

Remove the cores from the apples. Take a knife and make a slit in the skin all round each apple, just above the middle.

Combine the sugar, hazelnuts, raisins, cacao and cinnamon.

Place the apples on a baking tray and stuff the centres with the fruit and nut mix. Finish each apple with a squeeze of orange juice.

Bake for 20–25 minutes or until the apples are soft.

Willie's Tip: This is a store-cupboard dessert – use whatever dried fruit you have.

'I'll show you how to make tartuffo!' This is the chocolate dish
that my great friend Marco Pierre White so proudly taught me.
It's a magnificent dessert that would grace any dinner party,
and it's a wonderful way to taste the flavour notes of the chocolate.
It's also easy to make and can be made the day before.

Tartuffo

(Serves 12)

180g cacao, finely grated
300ml double cream
150g icing sugar
4 tbsp water

Line a 20cm loose-bottomed cake tin or small loaf tin with cling film.

Melt the cacao by placing it in a large heatproof bowl set over a pan of
simmering water.

Meanwhile, make a syrup with the caster sugar and water by heating them
gently in a small pan for a few minutes until the sugar has dissolved. Allow to
cool slightly.

Beat the cream until it forms soft peaks. Then gradually beat in the sugar
syrup.

Add a tablespoon of the cream mixture to the melted cacao and stir in well,
then gently fold the rest in. Pour the mixture into the cake or loaf tin
refridgerate until firm. Slice and serve with seasonal berries.

Willie's Tip: Lining the tin with cling film will help you to remove the
tartuffo from the tin. Leaving the melted cacao to cool slightly means that the
cream won't collapse when the cacao is added to it.w

The success of chocolate mousse is based entirely on the quality of the chocolate or cacao you use. You have to use a chocolate that's going to leap out at you to really make this work!

Chocolate Mousse

(Serves 8)

180g cacao, finely grated
5 eggs, separated
75g golden caster sugar
200ml double cream

Melt the cacao by placing it in a large heatproof bowl set over a pan of simmering water.

Meanwhile, beat the egg yolks with the sugar until fluffy and pale.

Lightly whip the cream in a separate bowl.

Whisk the egg whites until firm in another bowl.

Stir the melted cacao into the egg yolk mixture. If the cacao and egg mix clumps together and looks grainy, add a little whipped cream and keep stirring.

Add the remaining whipped cream, then gradually fold in the egg whites. Divide the mousse between serving glasses and refrigerate until ready to serve.

We had so many bananas in Venezuela we hardly knew what to do with them. We were always trying out new recipes – this was one of the best. In Devon, we serve it with double cream.

Baked Banana with Rum and Cacao

(Per person)

1 ripe banana, peeled
3 tsp finely grated cacao
3 tsp soft muscovado sugar
3 tsp dark rum
Juice (with pips) of half a passion fruit
Large knob of butter

Preheat the oven to 180°C (fan).

Place the banana on a small sheet of foil and pull the edges up slightly. Sprinkle with the cacao, sugar, rum and passion fruit juice and put the butter on top.

Seal the edges of the foil tightly and bake for 20–25 minutes.

Serve at once, straight out of the foil, with some cream or vanilla ice cream spooned on top.

I love fondue, so one day I came up with this recipe to take advantage of the abundance and variety of fruit at El Tesoro. I thread the fruit on to skewers and freeze them before dunking in the fondue. The cold fruit cools the chocolate so that it forms a case; it's like eating fruit chocolates. The kids love it and it's great fun to eat.

Chocolate Fondue

(Serves 8)

2 bananas, roughly chopped
250g strawberries
150g raspberries
180g cacao, finely grated
150g caster sugar
560ml double cream

Thread the fruit on to skewers and freeze.

When ready to eat, heat the cream and sugar in a pan until the sugar has dissolved. Add the grated cacao and stir until melted and combined.

Transfer the fondue to a fondue pot and serve with the frozen fruit for dunking.

When I think about the desserts I loved most as a child, I always picture my mum's bread and butter pudding, which she made in Ireland using her homemade bread. It was always such a treat to hit a plump sultana! In Venezuela, with cloud forest sugar, nutmeg trees on the lawn and the finest cacao at hand, this is what I gave my children. It's especially good made with cacao bread (page 132).

Bread and Butter Pudding

(Serves 6–8)

5 slices thin brown bread or cacao
   bread, spread with unsalted butter
50g sultanas or raisins, soaked in
   rum overnight, then drained
¼ tsp ground cinnamon
¼ tsp freshly grated nutmeg

2 heaped tbsp finely grated cacao
450ml whole milk
2 eggs
1 tsp vanilla extract
75g muscovado sugar

Lightly grease a 25cm square baking dish.

Cut the bread into triangles and lay half of the pieces, butter-side down, in the dish. Sprinkle over half the sultanas, cinnamon, nutmeg and cacao. Top with the remaining bread, butter-side up, and the remaining fruit, spices and cacao.

Pour the milk into a pan and gently bring to just under the boil, then remove from the heat.

Whisk the eggs with the vanilla extract and 50g of the sugar. Stir in the hot milk and pour over the bread. Leave the bread to soak up the custard for 1 hour.

Preheat the oven to 180°C (fan).

Push any corners of bread that protrude too much down into the custard, sprinkle the pudding with the remaining sugar and place the dish in a roasting tin. Pour in enough boiling water to come halfway up the side of the dish. Bake for 25–30 minutes or until golden brown. Serve warm.

Back in England with no mangoes to forage, I happily settled down to blackberries and apples. Adding cacao to the crumble takes the countryside flavours of this classic English dish to new heights.

Blackberry and Apple Cacao Crumble

(Serves 6)

For the fruit:
1.5kg apples, peeled, cored
  and sliced
300ml blackberry juice (made from
  750g fresh blackberries, blitzed,
  then sieved)
100g muscovado sugar

For the cacao crumble:
225g plain flour
125g unsalted butter
125g muscovado sugar
50g ground almonds
50g finely grated cacao

Preheat the oven to 180°C (fan). Lightly grease an oval baking dish, about 25 x 30cm in size.

For the fruit mixture, put the apples, blackberry juice and sugar in a pan and heat gently for 8–10 minutes. Spoon into the dish and allow to cool.

For the crumble, put the flour, butter, sugar and almonds into a food processor and blitz until the mixture looks like fine breadcrumbs. Add the cacao and blitz to combine.

Top the cooled fruit with the crumble and bake for 35–40 minutes or until golden. Serve warm.

This is one of those dishes that reflects the season and where you live. Whether you throw in tropical fruits or raspberries, blueberries and strawberries, this is always a big hit with the kids.

Pavlova

(Serves 8)

For the meringue:
5 egg whites
275g golden caster sugar
1 tbsp white wine vinegar
2 tsp cornflour
1 tsp vanilla extract

For the filling:
250ml double cream
50g golden caster sugar
60g cacao, finely grated
2 passionfruit
tropical fruit, to decorate (such as
    starfruit, mango and papaya)

Preheat the oven to 120°C (fan). Line a baking tray with non-stick baking paper. Beat the egg whites with a pinch of salt until satiny peaks form. Gradually beat in the sugar. Fold in the vinegar, cornflour and vanilla extract.

Mound the meringue onto the baking tray and use wet fingers to flatten the top. Bake for 1–1¼ hours. Turn the oven off and leave the pavlova in it to cool completely.

Prepare the filling by gently heating the cream and sugar until just about boiling.
Stir in the cacao and remove from the heat. Transfer to a bowl and place in the refrigerator until cool but not solid.

Cut the passion fruit in half and push the pulp through a sieve into a bowl. Discard the seeds. Fold the pulp into the cacao cream.

Remove the pavlova from the baking paper and place on a serving plate. Pile on the cacao cream and top with the tropical fruits. Serve.

Cacao lifts crème caramel to new heights!

Chocolate Caramelo

(Makes 6)

180g caster sugar
150ml whole milk
300ml single cream
75g cacao, finely grated
4 eggs

Preheat the oven to 150°C (fan).

Prepare the caramel by putting 150g of the sugar into a pan along with 2 tablespoons of water. Heat gently until the sugar dissolves. Continue cooking until the syrup is a golden caramel colour. Divide the caramel between 6 x 125ml ramekins. Swirl around to coat, then set aside to cool.

Pour the milk and cream into a pan. Add the cacao, then bring just to the boil, stirring to melt the cacao.

In a small bowl, beat the eggs lightly with the remaining sugar. Pour the warm cream mixture into the eggs and stir well. Pour the mixture into the ramekins, then place them in a large roasting tin. Pour in enough hot water to come two-thirds of the way up the sides of the ramekins. Bake for 30–35 minutes until firm but with a wobble. Cool, then chill until ready to serve.

To serve, loosen each one with a knife and invert on to a plate.

I love meringues, but I always feel like they're missing something. For me, cacao provides the missing link.

Chocolate Meringues

(Makes 12)

4 egg whites
200g golden caster sugar
50g cacao, roughly chopped

Preheat the oven to 120°C (fan). Line a couple of baking trays with non-stick baking paper.

Whisk the egg whites and sugar together until stiff, shiny and firm. Fold in the cacao. Spoon the mixture on to the baking trays in 12 dollops, then use the back of a spoon to smooth off the tops.

Bake for 1 hour or until set, then switch off the oven and leave them inside to cool with the oven door open.

This is a fantastic accompaniment to cheese – and it's so good that you might forget to eat the cheese! The saltier the cheese, the better – manchego is fantastic.

Quince Chocolate Cheese (Membrillo)

(Makes 1kg)

1kg quinces, washed and halved
800g golden caster sugar
100g cacao, finely grated

Preheat the oven to 170°C (fan). Line a large loaf tin with non-stick baking paper.

Place the quinces on a baking tray, cover with foil and bake for 1½ hours or until soft and collapsing.

Deseed and push the quinces through a sieve with the back of a wooden spoon. Tip the resulting purée into a large pan and add the sugar. Heat gently until the sugar has dissolved. Add the cacao, then bring slowly to the boil and cook gently for 50 minutes or until the mixture starts to pull away from the edges of the pan. Pour the mixture into the loaf tin, allow to cool, then place in the refrigerator to set firm.

Turn out of the loaf tin and slice to serve.

When you live in the tropics and you're surrounded by every type of lush, juicy and exotic fruit, the last thing you're going to do is go down to the supermarket and buy your kids a factory-made chocolate spread. This is a healthy version and children love it. There were so many different types of berries to experiment with – fruits you've never even heard of in the UK, with names like lulo and mamon – that we had a lot of fun playing around with this recipe. We made it with whatever was in season. And it's fantastic made with British berries too, especially blackberry, the prince of darkness, found in hedgerows everywhere in autumn.

Chocolate Berry Spread

(Makes about 500g)

250g berries, such as strawberries, raspberries or blackberries
100g golden caster sugar
2 tbsp water
125g cacao, finely grated

Prepare a fruit sauce by placing the berries in a food processor and blitzing until smooth. Push through a fine nylon sieve if you'd prefer a seedless spread. Set aside.

Tip the sugar and water into a small pan and heat gently until the sugar dissolves.

Add the cacao and continue to heat until emulsified, stirring regularly. Remove the pan from the heat and stir in the fruit sauce. Pour the spread into an airtight container, leave to cool, then store in the refrigerator.

Willie's Tip: Use whatever berries are in season. Serve spare fruit sauce with Cloud Forest Chocolate Cake (see page 172). It also makes great icing for cupcakes. The spread keeps in the refrigerator for up to a week.

This is walking snack food, made in slabs and broken into bite-sized pieces. It's nutty, naughty and nice – mountain power food at its best. It's also a great Christmas dish: serve with drinks.

Caramelised Mixed Nuts & Nibs

(Serves 8–10)

50g unsalted butter, softened
25g golden caster sugar
½ tsp cayenne pepper
250g mixed nuts, such as pecans, almonds, hazelnuts, pistachios
50g cacao nibs, crushed

Preheat the oven to 180°C (fan). Line a baking tray with non-stick baking paper.

Mix together the butter, sugar and cayenne pepper until well combined, then add the nuts and cacao nibs and stir through. Season with salt and black pepper.

Spread out the nut mixture in a single layer on the prepared baking tray. Bake for 5 minutes, then stir and cook for a further 5 minutes or until crisp. Remove and leave to cool before serving.

I came up with this brittle while trying to invent sweets for the children. We turned it into a sweet jungle adventure by riding up to San Pablo in the cloud forest on donkeys to bring back *papelón* (sugar). Any sugar will do, but unrefined is best, as its flavour goes so well with nuts and cacao.

Cacao Nut Brittle

(Serves 8)

50g cacao nibs, roasted
50g toasted flaked almonds
100g golden caster sugar
50g butter

Line a baking tray with a sheet of non-stick baking paper, then scatter over the cacao nibs and almonds.

Put the sugar, butter and a splash of water in a medium pan and place over a gentle heat. Stir continuously until the sugar dissolves. Increase the heat and boil for about 5 minutes or until the mixture turns a light golden brown. Stir occasionally to stop the caramel from sticking to the pan.

Pour the caramel evenly over the nibs and almonds and leave to cool completely.

Break the brittle up into big shards and serve over ice cream or as a petit four.

When I was searching for new types of cacao, I travelled with my cast-iron pot from hacienda to hacienda, making cacao and then truffles to find the flavour notes I was looking for. Truffles are fantastic. We make them every which way. Tania makes rum truffles, using beautifully fat raisins soaked in Venezuelan rum. The raisins absorb the rum and burst in your mouth when you eat them. Folded into the truffle mix, they produce an incredible cacophony of chocolate, rum and raisin flavours. Amazing.

(Makes about 40 truffles)

250ml double cream
150g caster sugar
180g cacao, finely grated
Cocoa powder, for dusting

Heat the cream and sugar in a small pan until almost boiling, ensuring it does not boil. Stir in the cacao, then remove the pan from the heat.

Transfer the truffle mixture to a plastic container. Cover and place in the refrigerator until cold and firm.

To shape each truffle, scoop a teaspoon of the mixture and roll quickly between your palms. Dust the truffles with cocoa powder and store in the refrigerator until ready to serve.

Willie's Tip: Rather than rolling the truffles by hand, you could put the mixture in a piping bag and pipe lengths on to a tray lined with greaseproof paper. Use a knife to trim the lengths into bite-sized pieces. Dipping the truffles in melted chocolate before dusting them in cocoa will also add a professional finish.

My sister Sein gave me this recipe many years ago and I would never make my mince pies any other way now. The cacao compliments all the deep, rich flavours beautifully.

Mince Pies

(Makes 24)

For the pastry:
280g plain flour
25g ground almonds
175g unsalted butter
85g golden caster sugar
Zest of 1 lemon
1 egg yolk
3 tbsp whole milk

For the mincemeat:
50g cacao, finely grated
3 apples, such as russet or cox, grated
100g semi-dried apricots, roughly chopped
100g sultanas
100g raisins
100g currants
1 tbsp each light brown and dark brown muscovado sugar
1 tsp each ground cinnamon, grated nutmeg and mixed spice
Zest and juice of 2 lemons or oranges
5 tbsp rum or calvados or Grand Marnier
5 tbsp cognac
2 tbsp olive oil
Icing sugar, to finish

Prepare the pastry by putting the flour and almonds into a food processor. Add the butter and pulse until it looks like very fine breadcrumbs. Sprinkle in the sugar and add the lemon zest, egg yolk and milk and pulse until the mixture starts to clump together. Tip the pastry mixture on to a board and gently squeeze until it comes together into a ball – add water if it feels dry. Wrap the pastry in cling film and chill for 30 minutes.

Preheat the oven to 190°C (fan). Roll out the pastry on a lightly floured surface to the thickness of few millimetres. Using a 7cm cutter, cut out 24 discs and use to line two 12-hole bun tins. Gather up and roll out the pastry again, and use a 6cm cutter for the lids.

To make the mincemeat, first mix the cacao and apple in a large bowl. Blitz the dried fruit together in a food processor and add to the bowl. Add all the other ingredients except the icing sugarand stir well. Spoon 1–2 teaspoonfuls into each pastry case, dampen the edge of the pastry bottom with water and sit a smaller pastry disc on top. Pierced each lid to allow steam to escape and bake for 12–15 minutes until golden brown. Cool on a wire rack. Finish with a dusting of icing sugar.

Willie's Tip: This makes more mincemeat than you need, but the leftovers keep well in the fridge for up to a couple of weeks, allowing you to make more pies on demand.

One day my mum mentioned in passing how she had been making some great fruit and nut bites using cacao. I didn't think much more about it until I tasted them. Zing! Delicious and healthy, they're the best energy snack going.

Anna's Jewel Bites

(Makes about 40)

180g cacao, roughly chopped
100g walnuts, hazelnuts or Brazil nuts, roughly chopped
100g sultanas or raisins, or a mixture
100g crystallised ginger (add 30g more if desired), sugar shaken off, chopped
1 tsp ground cinnamon
2 tsp vanilla extract, such as Madagascan
1 tbsp honey, if desired
Splash of rum or cognac

Line a small loaf tin with cling film.

Put the cacao in a large heatproof bowl set over a pan of simmering water. When it has melted, add the nuts, sultanas, raisins and ginger and stir until well coated. Then add the cinnamon, vanilla, honey (if you like) and rum or cognac and stir. Spoon the mixture into the lined tin, smooth the top and refrigerate overnight.

Using the cling film, lift the loaf out of the tin, peel away the cling film and chop into bite-sized pieces to serve.

How many times have you thought to yourself, I'd love a silky smooth, sublimely sexy chocolate sauce? Well, here it is. This works as a topping for almost any dessert, from fruit to pancakes, pavlova to chocolate fondue.

Chocolate Sauce

200ml whipping cream
80g caster sugar
100g cacao, grated
10g unsalted butter

Put the cream in a pan set over a low heat, then add the caster sugar and stir until dissolved.

Add the grated cacao and stir until melted. Finally, stir in the butter for a smooth, silky chocolate sauce. Serve warm.

Index

Page numbers in *italic* refer to illustrations

huevos rancheros 124
chococchino 122, *123*
chocolate *see* cacao and chocolate
chocolate and berry spread 208, *209*
chocolate and chicken liver pâté 148
chocolate biscuits 182, *183*
chocolate caramelo 204, *205*
chocolate corn cakes 134, *135*
chocolate cupcakes 174, *175*
chocolate factory, setting up 80–1, 84–94, 98, 100–8
chocolate flapjacks 177
chocolate fondue 198, *199*
chocolate meringues 206
chocolate mousse 196
chocolate nemesis 51–2, 83
chocolate pecan tart 184, *185*
chocolate sauce 218
The Chocolate Society 81, 84
Choroni 12–13, 24–5, 26, 40, 53, 99
Christmas cake, Willie's chocolate 98
Christmas Day traditions 99
Chuao cacao 17
churros 129
Cloud Forest chocolate cake 98, 108, 172, *173*
cocoa powder 32
coconut and cacao, fish curry with 154
Cody, Chantelle 83
Colonia Tovar *54*
Columbus, Christopher 30
conching 32, 85–6, *96*, 105–6
confectionery: cacao nut brittle 211
   caramelised mixed nuts and nibs 210
   truffles 212, *213*
coq au vin 162, *163*
corn on the cob: cachapas 134, *135*
Cortés, Hernándo 30
Costa Maya 55–7, 62, 77
crayfish 42
crème caramel: chocolate caramelo 204, *205*
Criollo beans 54–9, 106
crumble, blackberry and apple cacao 201
cucumber: gazpacho 138, *139*
Curley, William 105
currants: mince pies 214, *215*
curries 62
   fish curry with coconut and cacao 154
Cuyagua 32–4

D

dates and chocolate, with lamb tagine 164
deep, dark and delicious ice cream 188, *189*
desserts: baked apples 192, *193*
   baked bananas with rum and cacao 197
   blackberry and apple cacao crumble 201
   bread and butter pudding 200
   chocolate caramelo 204, *205*
   chocolate fondue 198, *199*
   chocolate meringues 206
   chocolate mousse 196

chocolate pecan tart 184, *185*
   deep, dark and delicious ice cream 188, *189*
   gooey chocolate puddings 190, *191*
   pavlova 202, *203*
   tartuffo 194, *195*
   tiramisu 186, *187*
dressing, cacao 152
drinks: alcoholic hotties 122
   Bloody Mary 130, *131*
   chococchino 122, *123*
   espresso choc shot 122, *123*
   hot choc chilli shot 122, *123*
   spiced hot choc 122, *123*
   Tania's hot chocolate 122, *123*
   Venezuelan hot chocolate 51, 100, 120, *121*
Dutching 32

E

eggs: huevos rancheros 124
   Willie's Venezuelan breakfast 99, 126–8, *126*
El Tesoro, Hacienda *see* Tesoro, Hacienda
Emmanuel 74–5
England, Willie moves back to 74–5, 80
espresso choc shot 122, *123*
Europe, introduction of cacao to 30

F

Felix 56–7, 77
Ferguson, Tom and Giana 20
fish curry with coconut and cacao 154
fishing 42
flapjacks, chocolate 177
fondue, chocolate 198, *199*
Francesci brothers 100–1
Freeman, Dean 23
French beans: Puy lentil and roast tomato
   salad 152, *153*
fruit: baked apples 192, *193*
   baked bananas with rum and cacao 197
   blackberry and apple cacao crumble 201
   chocolate berry spread 208, *209*
   chocolate fondue 198, *199*
   heavenly cheesecake 180, *181*
   pavlova 202, *203*
Fry, Joseph 32

G

game: partridge basted with cacao 166, *167*
   pheasant and cacao casserole 165
gazpacho 62, 138, *139*
Gentle-Cadeau, Linny 81–2, 105, 106
ginger: Anna's jewel bites 216, *217*
   junkie pig 160, *161*
gooey chocolate puddings 190, *191*
gravy, chicken cacao 168
Gray, Rose 83
grue de cacao 116
guasacaca 26

Acknowledgements

I'm indebted to all the friends and family and countless others, both here and in Venezuela, who have supported me over the years. Without them none of this would have been possible. But there are some people who deserve a special mention, and without whom Willie's Cacao and the series and thus this book would not have seen the light of day.

In Venezuela there is Arturo Sarmiento whose support I couldn't have done without. And Alfredo Astadiurraga, Alexandra de Yavorsky and Teling Arnal who have proved invaluable. Ricardo and Annabel Soto, Betilio Araujo and the boys have looked after the farm as if it was their own. John Kehoe is the man who bought the first beans I ever sold, and many years later brokered the first export that started Willie's Cacao. I'm ever grateful to San Jose Cacao and especially to the Franchesci family.

Back in England there is a wonderful team including: Marco Pierre White, a great friend and adviser; Dean Freeman, who is instrumentally supportive; Spencer Buck, Alex Bane, Ryan Wills and the rest of the team at Taxi Studio; Jim Bell and Gary Bell at Haas-Tek Services for all their help; Tom Vogel, my great American adviser; Robert Smith who was always there to help; Jim Bellini, the catalyst for so much and an old friend; Sarah Ball who gave many hours to sourcing machines in Spain; William Aldous, full of factual chocolate information; Bob 'the builder' Browning; Eddie Cheeseman at Final Cut who took on another man's dream; Chris More at Waitrose for believing in Willie's Cacao; Selfridges for launching Willie's Cacao, and especially Ewan Venters; Reapers of Tiverton who have sold a lot of bars for a small shop; Mariela, Kamila and Agnieszka, the girls who work tirelessly in the factory; Jake Nava, a solid friend; Mark Darlington and Toby Anderson who put tunes to the original taster; Brian King who helped greatly with my old machines – a master welder; Twyfords who gave us precision engineering; Peter Woodman and Paul Langdon at Finds who always lent a hand; Terry's Joinery who were always there to help at Langlands.

At Liberty Bell/Doris who made the television series, my thanks go especially to David Buckley, Stuart Prebble, Sam Richards, Southan Morris, Emma Robertson and Eli Hardy. To my publishers, Hodder & Stoughton, I must thank a fabulous team who have all believed in me, including Nicky Ross, Alice Wright, Sarah Hammond, Camilla Dowse, Bill Jones and Zelda Turner who edited the book, for which I'm immensely grateful. Katie Giovanni was our home economist; Will Webb designed the pages, and Christian Barrett did the incredible photography. Thanks to Ceramica Blue (www.ceramicablue.co.uk), and last but by no means least a huge thanks to Rebecca Cripps, a pleasure to work with and a great friend. I'm extremely grateful to my agents, LAW, and especially to Araminta, the best agent.

Finally, and most significantly, I must thank my family – my father, who taught me so much and gave me the skills to put together the machinery and build the chocolate factory; Mum and Henry and the rest of my family, Arabella, Sein, Sophie, Jessie, Harry and Dolly for their great support. And at the last, a special thanks to my children, Sophia, William and Eve, and to my wife, Tania, without whom nothing would be possible. This has been a long, hard road, and she has held everything together with unwavering support and love. Thank you.